THE CAMINO DE SANTIAGO: ONE WANDERFUL WALK

SHANNON O'GORMAN

ISBN: 978-1-7368010-3-1 (Paperback edition)

ISBN: 978-1-7368010-4-8 (E-book edition)

To my parents, for starting me on the right path in the beginning

FOREWORD

To write this book I relied on a blog that I kept while walking the Camino de Santiago in April and May of 2019. I have changed the names of characters in this book with the exception of my sister, Sharlene, who completed this journey with me. I took some liberties with dialogue when I could not recall the exact words. In addition to my memory and blog entries, I have included researched facts when I felt they added to the depth and understanding of the story.

0 10   50km

Fisterra

Olveira

Negreira

O Pedrouzo

Arzúa

Palas de Rei

Santiago de Compostela

Sarria

Portomarín

Triacastela

O Cebreiro

Ponferrada

Villafranca del Bierzo

Rabanal del Camino

Hospital de Orbigo

Mansilla

ATLANTIC OCEAN

Porto

PORTUGAL

ES

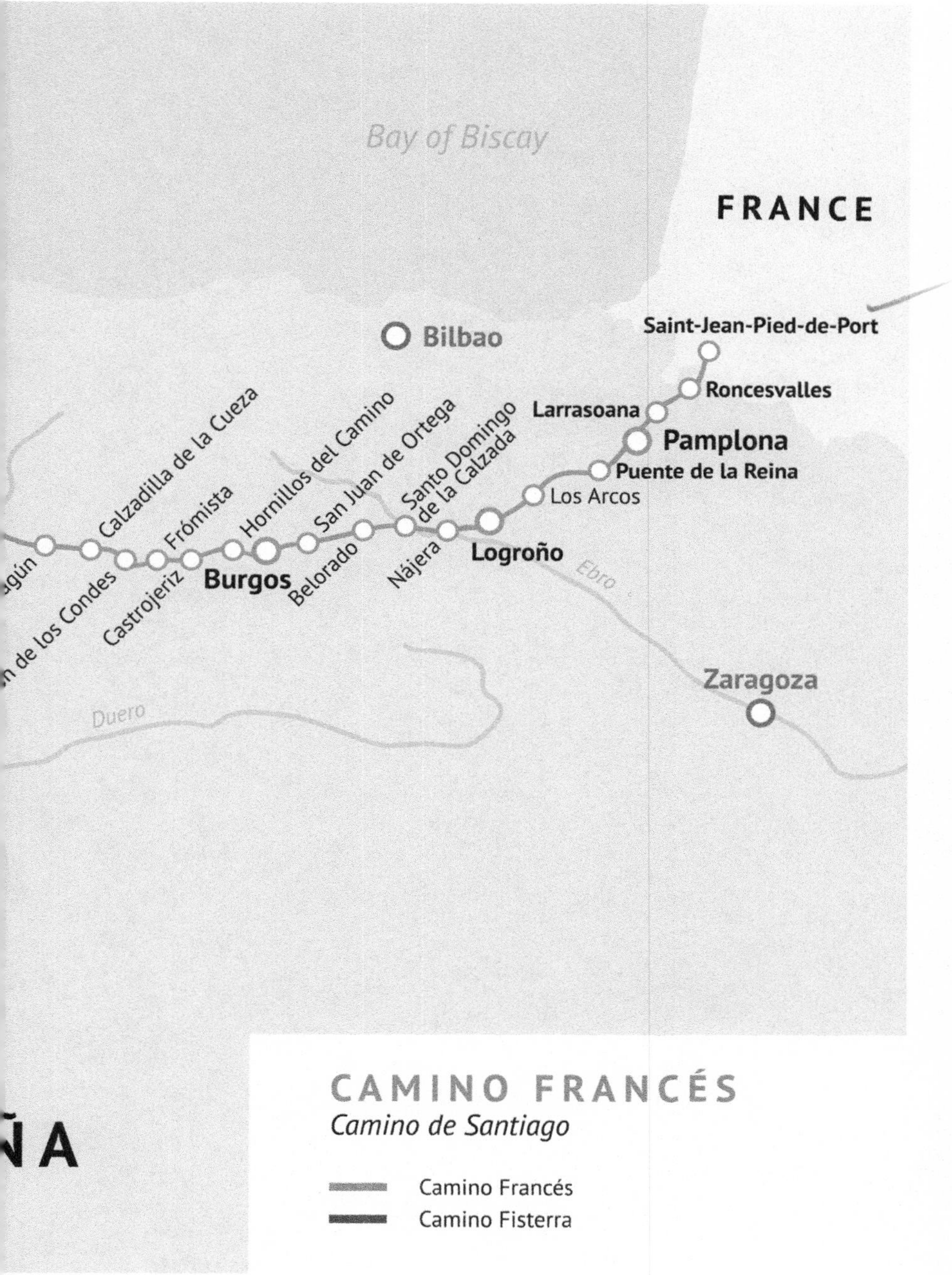

Bay of Biscay

FRANCE

○ Bilbao

Saint-Jean-Pied-de-Port
○ Roncesvalles
Larrasoana ○
Pamplona
Puente de la Reina
Calzadilla de la Cueza
Hornillos del Camino
San Juan de Ortega
Santo Domingo
de la Calzada
Frómista
Los Arcos
...gún ○
de los Condes
Castrojeriz
Burgos
Belorado
Nájera
Logroño
Ebro

Zaragoza
○

Duero

CAMINO FRANCÉS
Camino de Santiago

━━━ Camino Francés
━━━ Camino Fisterra

ÑA

CONTENTS

INTRODUCTION

"The journey of a thousand miles begins with a single step." – Lao Tzu

I took a walk once, down long dusty roads, across farmers' fields, onto half-deserted cobblestoned streets, past old watchful stone buildings, through cities with used car lots and polluted air, and over green pastures where the air hung heavy with the scent of wildflowers and cow dung. It was called the Camino de Santiago. It has been tread upon by millions of people who have left a bit of themselves in each footstep, to be picked up by another and passed on and on. Some parts of this path are narrow and winding, some are old straight Roman roads, some parts climb up to touch the sky, and other parts push roughly down over loose gravel and crumbling earth. It is a way of faith and disbelief. It is a road that will test your body, mind, and soul. It will torture you and nurture you. It will tickle your soul if you let it. It is one 'wanderful' walk that you will never forget.

Some people walk it hoping for an epiphany or a great flash of clarity about themselves, their faith, and the world. But, you can walk it without any expectations, with just an open mind and open heart and no pressure to change yourself. You will meet people walking because they like to walk, talking because they like to talk, and stopping because they want to stop. You can walk to get fit or to appreciate the beauty of the landscape, the architecture, and the magnificent culture. You can walk to remember or to forget, or to just pass the time.

You can make deep, meaningful connections with people as you walk. Or, if you desire solitude, you can walk alone and be at peace with yourself. You can share stories and meals in smaller albergues (hostels) or stay in a larger, luxurious hotel with a deep bath.

You may encounter bed bugs, blisters, illness, or injury, or you may not. Listen to your body, but believe in yourself. Just like learning a language, you can learn from your mistakes.

Ultimately, this walk, this pilgrimage, this journey, is a profoundly personal experience that is different for everyone. But, some things are the same for everyone; walk, eat, sleep and repeat. It will give a nice rhythm to your day.

A sense of humor, flexibility and a burning desire to reach Santiago de Compostela are what can help so many complete this journey.

Historically, the Camino de Santiago is a thousand-year-old pilgrimage route that stretches westwards nearly 500 miles over the Pyrenees towards the relics of St. James the Apostle in the city of Santiago de Compostela in northwest Spain. Known in Spain as 'peregrinos' (pilgrims), people walk on foot (some in expensive footwear and some barefoot), bicycle or horseback or any way they can imagine. They set off from various points to walk west each day. How far they get is up to them. They may have pre-booked accommodation, or they may just see how far they want to walk each day.

Once they have found a place to stay, they show their pilgrim's passport. This small booklet is used for collecting ink stamps from accommodations, cafes, or shops. Albergues allow pilgrims with this special passport to stay the night at a low cost, usually in a shared dormitory-style room. The price is usually between 5-20 euros. Certain accommodations (donativo) even accept a "donation" where you can pay what you want.

Pilgrims can now also download the mobile application 'Credencial del Peregrino.' Through this app, you can get the digital stamps necessary to prove your pilgrimage to Santiago. These digital stamps can be obtained through the QR codes available at the different points of the Camino de Santiago. The paper pilgrim credential will continue to be accepted as well.

The Camino de Santiago winds through hills, mountains, towns, and cities and is marked with signs or yellow arrows. It is the ultimate treasure hunt! But, if you don't think you can find all the markings, or you are worried about getting lost, there is always GPS tracking on your phone. Of course, everyone in Spain knows where the Camino runs, so you could always ask a local. You never know what conversation could result from that!

All those who complete the journey will receive a Compostela. This is a certificate of completion for the pilgrimage and makes a nice reward for finishing their journey. Even those on a short route from Sarria (about 100 miles) who have received two unique paper or digital stamps for each day of their walk can also receive a special Compostela.

Some people may have walked for religious reasons, some for health or touristic reasons, so there are different kinds of Compostelas. What is not different, though, is the feeling of completion each pilgrim will have, despite the distance traveled or the reason for the walk.

Whatever the reason, be it secular or spiritual, whether they are escaping life, walking to forget, walking to discover, or looking for a reason to be alive, each person is on their own journey. Some may not know why they have come to walk, and others may discover the reason through the rhythm of their steps. Perhaps there is no reason at all, just a simple curiosity and a belief that they are doing something they want to do.

Young parents can be seen pushing children along the way in baby carriages. Some people jog. Some people cycle. Some are very young, and some are in their 90s. Some walk arm in arm, and some walk single-file. Everyone walks west.

Many people have done more than one Camino. Some people have waited all their life for the opportunity to do their first Camino. Perhaps people do a section of the Camino and come back another year to do another section. If they have the time, the entire Camino de Santiago from St Jean Pied de Port takes about a month to complete.

There are other Camino routes, too, that also end in Santiago. Up near San Sebastian is the Camino Norte; a route called the Camino Portuguese starts in Porto, and a longer route starts in Le Puy, France. Even more routes exist; they are not as popular, but if you wish to see fewer people, they may be for you.

Some of the appeal of The Camino de Santiago, The Way of St. James (The French Way), also has to do with the excellent network of accommodations, shops, restaurants, bars, small towns, and cities that this route passes through. You don't need to carry food with you, and you can even ship your backpack ahead each day to your albergue, should you not want to carry it. A lot has changed since pilgrims walked this route a thousand years ago, but many things have not changed at all.

As a kid, I used to think of myself as a bit of a fortune-teller. I'd look at someone's palm and examine the lines seriously.

Then, I would make up a fabulous story about their future. Many of these readings would have my 'customer' traveling far, far away, or having many children and living happily ever after. The lines led wherever I decided.

When I heard about the 500-mile walk on the Camino de Santiago, I found myself inexplicably staring at my palm once again. I wasn't thinking about my lifeline or my love line, though. Instead, I imagined different Camino paths in the palm of my hand. The Camino Norte, at the top of my palm. The Portuguese Camino up one side and the Le Puy Camino and the Via de la Plata up another. But, ultimately, I decided to take the main path across my palm, the Camino de Santiago, The Way of St. James (The French Way). I would see where it led me. And, that path was the one more traveled, and I think it made all the difference (apologies to Robert Frost!).

I decided not to walk with a donkey (like the author Tim Moore) or an angry family member. I couldn't convince anyone to go with me, and I didn't want to deal with all that pouting anyhow. I didn't have to visit any previous lives (Shirley MacLaine) or look for deep spiritual insight (Paulo Coelho). That German comedian (Hape Kerkeling) had written a funny book about lots of drinking and unusual situations. I supposed that could happen to me too, but I decided to do what most people did, throw a pack on my back, just walk and see what happened.

I did some research and some shopping. I bought books on various Caminos, some old, some new, and started to think. Some Camino books I read were the accounts of older female pilgrims dealing with bad knees. Some were the accounts of young men on bicycles burning quickly across the land or others pulling a cart slowly behind them.

In some books, they wove the legends of each area into the story. There were also fictional books about murder and mayhem on the Camino and quests for hidden treasure. It seemed that the Camino really did provide!

Long before all the modern-day guidebooks, memoirs, and fictionalized accounts, another book existed, the Codex Calixtinus, a juicy jam-packed book of liturgy, history, and a guide for the pilgrim in the Middle Ages. There were maps, descriptions, inn names, information on drinking water sources, and food. (All those years before Lonely Planet!) The pilgrimage route could be dangerous, and this information helped act as a useful guide. Around the 12th century, half a million pilgrims with sore feet were walking to Santiago. What a business opportunity for so many!

These days, the book most used on the route is undoubtedly John Brierley's, *A Pilgrim's Guide to the Camino de Santiago.* This masterpiece of Camino guidance has details of history, maps, accommodation, cafes, and restaurants. People are often spotted with this guidebook open in cafes or stopped on the path in quiet contemplation about which route to take next or where to stay at night. It's nice to arrive at a place to stay before darkness falls.

It must have been so very different on the Camino many years ago. There was no calling ahead for reservations. People would have walked day and night to get as far as they could. Ordinary people would have looked up at the stars to stir their minds. (Twinkle twinkle little star. How I wonder what you are?)

For the first pilgrims on the Camino, around the early Middle Ages, the twinkling stars were like terrestrial shepherds, accompanying them along a spiritual journey that would have been dramatically different from their everyday lives. So far away from their lives working in fields, the Camino gave them an opportunity for self-reflection. What did they think about as they walked to the end of The earth? New shoes? Where to find the best inn with the cheapest mead closest to the pilgrimage route? Cute pilgrims of the opposite sex? An all-inclusive breakfast option?

The stars sprawled across the night sky would have been their navigation guide, or possibly even a chance to interact with the deep thoughts of creation. Did they find God along the Way? They would have survived many hardships to get to their destination of Santiago (San Iago is the Galician translation of St. James) de Compostela (Campus Stellae from the Latin for "field of stars").

Once they arrived, they could see the relics of St. James and get a plenary certificate to forgive their sins under the field of stars. For the early pilgrims, the destination was perhaps more important than the journey itself. In our present day, it is the journey, with the unique scenery, culture, new friendships, and the opportunity for self-discovery that define the Camino for so many.

No matter how different our lives are from those who first traveled the Camino, the basic aspects of the journey remain fully intact. Maybe the Camino can have an even more significant impact today because it provides an escape from the manufactured creations that dominate our lifestyles. Finally, there is a chance to disconnect with the perpetual doom-scrolling of the news many of us now do all day long.

In our modern lives, the stars are muted by the city lights, often leaving us without the starry connection from years gone by. Disconnecting from our urban life with its emphasis on technology, the Camino lets us follow the cosmos so that we can try to forget about our lives back home. The journey ultimately draws our hidden aspirations to the surface and lets us consider the eternal walk under the stars that so many have done and have yet to do. Each step can be a thought, even if it is "How the heck did I get another blister?"

~

March 2019, San Jose, California. A bright, sunny Sunday morning. I'm sipping a hot milk coffee in a big blue mug on my deck, birds are chirping, bite-sized green hummingbirds are whirring around sniffing flowers, squirrels are racing for control along the thick black hydro lines, neighbors are swearing about being late for church, and cars are honking nearby on the El Camino Real. This is the old Spanish Road, the Royal Road that connected the 21 Spanish missions in California. It's been replaced as the primary artery by highways but clotted rusty bronze bells still mark the way with the sign–Historic El Camino Real. I'm leaving for France in the morning to walk on another Camino, the Camino de Santiago.

For the past month, I've walked to some California missions near me to prepare for the adult version of 'Mother May I' take a giant step into the unknown. One day I walked to Mission Santa Clara on the grounds of the beautiful Santa Clara University. Another day I walked to Mission San Jose, about a 5-hour walk amidst tech companies and asphalt.

Feeling inspired by my walks, I decided to walk from San Jose to San Francisco, a distance of about 50 miles. I would end my mini-Camino at the Mission Delores in San Francisco. I split this up a bit and did it over three weekends. One Sunday, I walked to Menlo Park, another Sunday I took the Caltrain to Menlo Park and then walked as far as Burlingame, and the last Sunday I took the Caltrain to Burlingame and then to Mission Delores in San Francisco. It had felt great to get to my destination, and it made me quite confident that I was making the right choice in going to Spain to walk the Camino de Santiago. (It also made me realize that perhaps I should do more training on hills. Some of those elevation gains in San Francisco were challenging too!)

I continued to walk a lot (sometimes up hills on weekend hikes) and continued to read a lot about the Camino. I found out quite a bit about St James before I left. He was one of the twelve original Apostles and was sent on a community outreach program to Spain to preach to the masses in the Northwest part of Spain called "Finis Terrae" The End of the World. Imagine people were even yelling fake news then! Things didn't go that well for James, and he was recalled to Jerusalem and had his head chopped off. Was this the beginning of cancel culture?

The historical details get a bit murky but, according to some accounts, the rest of his body was put in a boat and eventually washed up on the shores of Northern Spain and was hidden away for 800 years until a shepherd discovered the tomb under a shining light (though how was it identified without a head is a mystery?). A Bishop confirmed the find (from the tibia or the femur?), and perhaps recognizing the benefits of mass tourism, a beautiful chapel and later a Cathedral was constructed in Santiago. The bones were interred inside, and Santiago became the third most important pilgrimage site after Jerusalem and Rome.

Pilgrims, hearing of the miracle, began to walk to Santiago, The Way of St. James, to see the relics and even get a Planetary Indulgence certificate—a document stating that all their sins were forgiven. Just like that! By the 12th and 13th centuries, pilgrims were shuffling down the route staying in small inns, barns (the first real fresh-air Airbnbs), haggling in souvenir shops, and probably sipping mead in smelly outdoor cafes. The Templar Knights stepped in to offer their protection services, and the people just kept coming!

Other relics were displayed in churches along the way, maybe a saint's finger, another body part, hair, fingernails, clothing, anything attached to someone holy. Some believed that by being close to a relic, perhaps even touching or kissing it; a miracle could occur. There were many things to see along the route of the spiritual quest for the pilgrims, no doubt both strengthening faith for some and weakening it in others. It was a challenging route, with many getting sick, being robbed, or even dying. Pilgrims' hospitals were set up in many places along the way to help with sore feet and illness. And once they got to Santiago, they still had to walk all the way back.

I was only planning on walking one way. I'd need good shoes. I purchased a pair of cheap shoes, which was not my best decision in retrospect. I bought a few new hiking shirts, a jacket, a raincoat, a couple of pairs of pants and followed people's suggestions of keeping the pack weight to 10 percent of your body weight. I stuffed everything into a backpack with a small sleeping bag, some toiletries, and a small first aid kit. It still felt cumbersome. Where was I going to put all my souvenir relics?

And so I flew to Paris and hung out for a day, sucking in the sweet and stale French air and plenty of fumes before I headed out into the fields, the hills, and the mountains of Spain. In Paris, I located Shakespeare and Co., a bookshop which was a bucket list visit for me. The bookshop had large picture-perfect green and yellow trim and awnings, books on sale tables out front table, and a couple of benches to sit on and stare wistfully out at the Seine and Notre Dame.

The original bookstore had been the hang-out of Ernest Hemingway, F. Scott Fitzgerald, James Joyce, and other members Lost Generation tribe. I love Kerouac, especially his novel *On the Road*, and felt it was pretty fitting to be in the shop before starting my journey.

I bought a copy of *On the Road* and stuffed it in my backpack back at my affordable little hotel on Rue Daguerre near Montparnasse station. I had a copy of James Michener's *Iberia* downloaded on my phone. I'd always been interested in traveling to Spain since I'd read it.

It's incredible how books and even movies can influence our decisions. Watching the movie, *The Way*, with Martin Sheen walking the Camino, was also a big motivator for me to walk the Camino. The scenery looked so darn fantastic. If Martin Sheen and Shirley MacLaine could do it, so could I!

I wondered what stories I would hear on the road of the Camino. Its history was so full of St James's miraculous return to Spain, but I had read accounts of many more modern-day miracles on the Camino. I had read the stories of witches, The Templar Knights, and a few Camino legends. The Camino was a journey for the body, mind, and soul, and I hoped I was ready!

PROLOGUE

Early morning at Montparnasse station, I crammed a warm croissant into my mouth, chased it down with an espresso shot, and jumped onto a train headed for Bayonne and then another to St Jean. This second train was a cute blue and yellow two-car train, and I thumped down in a free seat beside a thirtyish woman who was thumbing through her copy of a Camino guidebook. I had been planning to spend a few hours in Bayonne, but it was raining hard, so I made a split-second decision to continue to St Jean. This involved running back to the ticket office, getting another ticket, and jumping through the train door just as it closed. A little luck was a good thing.

Most of the seats were filled with people of all ages with shimmering colorful backpacks, sleeping bags, walking poles, and rain ponchos. Everyone was chatting, laughing, and smiling. They were not your everyday tired-out commuters! We were all going to the same place on that train clattering down the tracks. St Jean. It almost sounded like I could hear the echo of Camino, Camino, Camino, as we went down the tracks.

I caught my breath for a second and glanced over at my seat-mate. She was reading John Brierley's book. I'm sometimes quite a shy person, but I had decided that if I was going to do this walk, I was going to have to really "put myself out there." Now was as good a time as any to start.

"Hi," I said. "I guess everyone reads that book."

"Yes," she smiled back at me. "I used it on my first Camino, and it saved me many times."

"Oh, when did you do the first one?"

"About four years ago. I've been trying to get back ever since. I'm Marie, by the way."

We chatted the entire short train ride to St. Jean. I learned how to pronounce Ron-ces-Val-les, where I was planning on spending my 2nd night. Marie was a social worker in Amsterdam and was back for some R and R from her stressful job. I felt fortunate to be able to "pick her brain" about St Jean, and before we knew it, we had arrived.

I followed Marie and the rest of the train gang uphill and onto the main cobblestone street where the pilgrim office was. It was about 1 pm, and the office was closed, but about 15 of us stood in line waiting in the light rain. Ponchos on, umbrellas open, and excitement levels cranked way up.

When the door was unlocked, we filed inside and waited in line until it was our turn to sit at a table. There was a long row of tables staffed by volunteers. Many different languages were being spoken, and everyone was excited. The volunteers called out "English! Francais! Espagnol!" and I went to an English speaker and received a paper with accommodation information.

"The Napoleon route is closed because of heavy snow. It is not possible to go to Orisson now. The Valcarlos route is very beautiful, though, and it will be open tomorrow," a volunteer told me.

"OK, thanks." It didn't really matter which route I took, but I did feel a little sad for some reason.

I knew the Valcarlos route was a gentler, winding path around the mountain and not just up and over. There would be some stretches beside the highway, but that was okay with me. I was a little disappointed that I couldn't go to Orisson (a sort of halfway stop before Roncesvalles on the Napoleon route), but it was probably for the best. I would have been following the same route that Napoleon had used to invade Spain all those years ago. The route was a tough uphill slog; was I really ready for that?

In the office, I also got my first stamp in my pilgrim credential. I had purchased it in advance online. The Canadian *credential* is available to members of the Canadian Company of Pilgrims who walk, cycle, or ride (horseback) the Camino. Other countries have their own credential, or you can simply get the credential at the Pilgrim office. I also bought a scallop shell here and tied it onto my backpack. This was the symbol of a pilgrim, and now everyone would know I was walking the Camino. As if anyone with a backpack would be doing anything different!

This whole stamp thing reminded me a lot of backpacking in the UK years ago, staying at YHA hostels and getting a stamp fo each night's accommodations also. Of course, then, you had to do chores like washing dishes or sweeping out dorms until you finally got the stamp. I hadn't heard of any Camino chores, but I was looking forward to sharing the experience with others, just like in the good old backpacker days.

"This really sucks," Marie told me as we walked out to the street together. "Last time, the Napoleon route was closed for me, too. Now, I will have to come back and do another Camino!"

I told Marie I'd see her later and went to find the accommodation I had booked for a night, Gite Makila. It wasn't hard to locate. It was on the main street, about a minute walk from the Pilgrim office. It was in a cute stone building and opened into what seemed to be a room of shoes in shoe boxes. A lot of them looked very new, much like mine. Would we all be doing a lot of "sole-searching" in the morning for the right pair along with the Camino soul searching? Only time would tell.

I met Pancho, the owner, who was a super friendly guy. He showed me to my bed, which had a red curtain that I could use for privacy. It was a perfect way to ease myself into sharing a room with others. There were only six beds in the room, and it seemed like only three other people were staying there. I found a nice lounge room on the 2nd floor with coffee and tea, soft drinks and beer available for a few euros. Nobody was around though, so I decided to head off and explore a little, too.

There were many, many *gites* on this main street. The lowest advertised price I saw on any sign was 8 euros in a dormitory. *Gites* are essentially hostels for hikers in France. In Spain, they were called *albergue*.

It was a beautiful little town of cobblestoned streets, small shops with hiker's clothing and souvenirs, and cute restaurants. There was a shop directly across from Gite Makila with all the supplies a pilgrim could desire. I bought some walking poles (they were supposed to remove 30% of the weight from your legs) and a pocket knife and resisted the urge to buy a scarf, a t-shirt, and a very funky black beret.

I continued to walk down to the river. The view of the rounded bridge was perfect, quaint, and picturesque. Beyond the center of town were lush green hills and low mountains. Everyone on the street seemed to have a silly grin on their face.

I took a few photos along the river and wandered back to the hostel where I met Lina, who was staying in the same room as me. She was from Germany, and it was her 3rd Camino. With her short brown hair, glasses, and tall thin build, Lina looked like someone I could depend on if need be.

An Israeli guy and South African woman showed up too, and we were all ridiculously excited for the morning! The Israeli guy was walking to lose weight, and the South African

4

woman had already tried to do two Caminos but had been injured early on both times. I hadn't even considered the fact that I might get injured!

"I need to sleep, so much," the South African woman moaned. "It takes such a long time to get here." She closed herself off in the little red nest, and that is the last time I ever saw her.

The Israeli guy lay in his bunk texting.

"Do you want to come out for dinner?" Lina and I asked him.

"No, thanks. I need to tell my wife I'm still okay." I was pretty sure he had only been away a day at the most.

"I guess it's just us!" and Lina and I hit the cobblestones.

We found a restaurant called Le Chaudron with a nice warm glassed-in sitting area and got to know each other a bit. I ordered a small steak and fries and a glass of red wine. It had been a long day!

"So, what do you do in Germany?" I asked her, nibbling on a thick, salty fry served in a cute little metal basket.

"I work for a medical supply company, but I've just retired. My husband and I are planning to ship a camper van to eastern Canada next year and drive through Canada and then the US and down to Mexico."

"Wow, that is quite an adventure! I've never even been to eastern Canada."

"Are you Canadian?" she asked excitedly.

"Yes, but I'm sorry," I said, "I'm trying not to be nice all the time!"

"Aw," Lina nodded, a bit confused, not quite getting my joke. I decided not to explain how Canadians are sometimes perceived as being nice or apologetic all the time.

Instead, I tried, "It's so true people never see their own countries. We always think there is a lot of time, but other places just seem more interesting."

"Yes, there are many parts of Germany that I have not

seen, but I don't want to. I would prefer to travel far away to see the beautiful nature in another country."

We chatted a bit more about travel, and I promised to tell her later what I knew about Eastern Canada (it wasn't much) and then walked back to the room. I hadn't seen Marie again, but I was sure I'd see her down the road. The other two in the room were already sleeping with their red curtains pulled around their beds.

I loved those little curtains; they gave you a bit of privacy. It was a nice, safe little cocoon before we would all burst out on the Camino in the morning.

I hoped the butterflies in my stomach would vanish by then.

PART I

SHEDDING-BALANCING YOUR BODY

1

STARTING OUT

DAY 1-ST JEAN PIED DE PORT TO RONCESVALLES-25 KM

"Head south where they speak French, cross the mountains through the pass at St Jean, walk until they speak Spanish, then keep the sun at your back in the morning, and in front of you in the afternoon, or by night, follow the stars known as the Milky Way until your reach the sea." - Codex Calixtinus

At 6:00 am, that auspicious morning in St Jean, I pulled back the thick red curtains around my little bed. It was showtime! I'd had a good sleep, but the rustling of plastic bags and things being pulled out of backpacks had woken me up. That was something I was going to have to get used to. My new black hiking pants and black shirt seemed unbelievably wrinkle-free as I pulled them on. I decided to pack up everything later and went upstairs to the sunny common room with a great book collection.

A long table with assorted bread and juices sat waiting under a large window that gave a great view of the distant green mountains we were soon to see much more close up.

It was a quick breakfast with about ten people—a perfect way to start. There was a lot of high energy at the table that morning. We were all fresh and wore our new Camino clothes. A young American woman was clad in what looked like the newest REI Peregrino fashion; nicely coordinated beige hiking pants, a light brown shirt, and a new Camino buff (a scarf/wrap that could double as a headband scarf, mask, or whatever).

"I'm doing the Camino in 22 days!" she announced to us all between power sips of an energy drink she had. "I plan to walk or jog at least 25 miles a day."

"Have you been training a lot?" someone asked.

"Not at all," she said. "It's not necessary for me. I'm only 25. I'll get used to the distance as I walk. I'm a fitness trainer; I do this for a living. Good luck, everyone, in case I don't see you again, haha!" And, with a swish of Gore-Tex, she was off.

"Guess we'll never see her again!" someone said. "In 22 days, I'll probably still be in Pamplona!"

We all laughed nervously but we were all a little daunted by the fact someone was planning on walking 500 miles in 22 days. I was on the 34-day plan.

After that quick breakfast, I went back to my room, stuffed things into my backpack, and grabbed my new hiking poles.

Then, I pulled down my shoes from the shoebox outside the room, laced them up carefully, and waited for Lina on the cool, dark street. God, I was excited!

"Ready, Shannon?" she asked.

"I've been ready for years!" I replied, clinking the tips of my walking sticks onto the cobblestones a few times like an excited puppy pawing at the earth.

It was still a little dark outside as we set off down the old road out of town. It felt surreal to be walking on the street I had seen in so many photos. Quite a few people were starting out, and the road was quiet except for the echoing click of walking poles, the smacking of boots on cobblestone, and the excited whispers and nervous laughter of other pilgrims. We stopped and took photos of ourselves, smiling, exhilarated, and looking very fresh! We left St Jean at about 7:00 am and followed the yellow arrows that marked the way out of town so very well.

The road weaved into the countryside, past small villages full of stone houses with green, red, and yellow window frames. Colorful flower pots decorated many of the windows; it was so darn quaint! Sometimes we walked beside the highway, and sometimes we saw an arrow beckoning across the highway, and we would madly dash across the road before a big semi-truck went barreling past. I hadn't prepared for traffic mania. (Perhaps I should have practiced running across the roads in San Jose more!) It all felt very close to that video game, Frogger, where you had to jump across traffic to reach safety.

Once on the other side of the highway, the route would cut across the country, perhaps following a stream uphill and getting close to some cows or sheep. We stopped for a rest in the town of Valcarlos and took in the views of the lush, green hills and mountains. We drank thick, strong coffee and took big hungry bites out of fresh croissants at a small table outside, chatting with other pilgrims and enjoying the view. We didn't linger too long; we were too excited to be walking.

"It's so beautiful already!"

"The fun has not begun for us today. It will become very difficult soon," some pessimistic American let us know.

Now I was worried things were going to get hard! But, at least we were not on the Napoleon route, which I knew had a lot more elevation.

I began to think a lot as I walked. What was up with my life? My daughter would be going to university soon, and my husband had a busy job with a tech company. I was an ESL teacher but had begun to work less and less. Should I completely retire? Maybe I could just keep doing Caminos every year?

There were not a lot of people on the path this morning so far. Our walking poles clicked on the highway and squelched quietly in the mud. It was a pretty tough walk, and it seemed to be mostly uphill, even though we were twisting around the mountain rather than going up and over.

The walking poles seemed like they had been a good idea already, as the road stretched out into the mountains and some snow appeared, and we had to watch our footing. At times, a rickety wooden fence blocked the possibility of an unplanned tumble down the hillside. The poles gave me an extra bit of support.

It began to rain lightly and then heavily (not on the first day, please!) and I was happy for some rain pants I had purchased. I stopped somewhere and pulled them on over my walking pants. I saw other people putting 'gaiters' on, which were kind of a fabric guard that stretched from your shoes to mid-calves. I hadn't bothered to buy any as I had the pants. You could purchase so many unnecessary things, and what did you really need except for a small pack and an ATM card?

Somewhere a coffee stop with a heater helped us all warm up a bit. As we climbed higher, snow covered some of the path, and it was very difficult in places. It became quite windy and snowy, but we all kept trudging on. I could see how the Napoleon route would have been hazardous to attempt. Even for us, it wasn't easy to see at times, and I had to put on a hat and gloves to stay warm.

Around 2:30, the large, white, stone monastery of Roncesvalles came into view and I breathed a little sigh of relief. People were lined up outside, cleaning the caked mud off their shoes and talking excitedly.

I hadn't known what to expect, but the accommodations were beyond my expectations. We formed an orderly line to get our pilgrim credential stamped and paid at the well-staffed reception desk. Hospitaleros (volunteers) patiently answered questions and stood around directing us to our dorm and telling us about the laundry or cooking facilities.

It was a beautiful place and had once an old medieval hospital for pilgrims walking long ago. It had been updated and was very modern now. I paid for a bunk (10 euros), breakfast (3.5 euros) and dinner (10 euros). I had no plans to walk any further looking for a restaurant.

The hot shower had good pressure and was separated into men's and women's. I got out of my damp clothes, finally. I literally felt like I could not walk another step.

There was also a very nice hotel attached to the monastery, for those who might want a more private experience.

Where I stayed in the monastery, bunks were spread out in a few rooms. My floor had spaces for about 60 people, with bunk beds organized into little pods of 4. An Italian man and his son were across from me, and no one was above me. There was a small outlet on the wall to charge my phone and a locker to put valuables in. At the desk, we had been warned not to leave phones charging unattended. It felt bizarre, but exciting, to be sleeping in a room with so many people.

I went exploring the monastery a little and found the

"chuck it or pluck it" (donation) table. Everyone who has done the Camino likely knows this table which is down the hall near the entrance. This is the place you empty your entire pack contents after that exhausting walk over the Pyrenees!

Anyways, I took a look to see if there was anything good, and I must say, there were plenty of panties and men's underwear. Like a lot. Were they that heavy? Hadn't everyone read about purchasing the lightweight ExOfficio briefs as I had? Also, there were blank journals, extra socks, lots of flashlights, extra shoelaces, umbrellas, adult diapers, a brand-new hairdryer, hats and gloves, and a lovely old Beatles shirt. I wanted that Beatles shirt badly, but I pulled my twitching fingers away. I decided not to leave anything on the table either. Although chucking my copy of *On The Road* was already tempting.

That pile of left-behind stuff on the table was entertaining, that was for sure. There were so many weird and wonderful things on it. There was even an entire set of foam hair curlers (who still used these?) left by someone who'd decided those hair rolls weren't worth the extra weight. I'd packed carefully but probably still had too much stuff.

While I had painstakingly found ways to lighten my pack (not bringing a clothesline and pegs had been a hard call), some people were actually adding things to their pack. Several ladies were picking up the socks and shoelaces and examining them. I'd still like to have a closer look at some things, but I didn't want to appear too eager either.

It was like a great free table at a garage sale, and as they say, "One man's junk is another man's treasure." On the Camino, I guess that translated to "One person's underwear could be yours if you act quick!"

Later on, coming back from picking up some clothes I had washed, I saw someone pick up the Beatles t-shirt. Damn! Was that underwear picked up, too? How about those rollers? I walked on by with incredible difficulty, not even wanting to imagine the fate of the adult diapers.

At 6:30, I presented my dinner voucher at the restaurant, and I was seated at a table with a talkative Danish couple. They were both very young, in their early twenties, and spoke very good English. Throughout the small restaurant, people were seated wherever there was a free chair at a table. Pasta, chicken, and carafes of wine were placed in the center of the table, and we helped ourselves. No one was alone, and there was a nice sense of camaraderie to celebrate the day.

My dinner companions were both university students who planned on walking the whole 500 miles as well. I liked these two a lot. They were bright and bubbly; he was the son of a minister, and she was an anthropology student. I didn't feel old talking to them. We all really clicked.

"Why are you guys walking?" I asked them.

"It's such a cliche. My dad wants me to find spiritual meaning in my life. But, the only spirit that I'm finding is this wine!" he added, laughing and filling up his glass. Yes, he actually said this!

"I just want to see if I can do it!" his girlfriend said.

That seemed as good a reason as any for walking the Camino.

"And, I told his dad that I would take care of him," his girlfriend added, also topping off her glass.

I was a little relieved that some of the first people I met were not on a quest for meaning. Instead, they were just walking to see if they could reach the end.

"Why are you walking?" the girl asked me.

"Like you guys, I want to see if I can do it. I want to see what happens!"

We had a little toast and congratulated ourselves that we were not "spiritual freaks." But, deep down, I wondered if I would be struck by divine insight along the Way. Beneath all the bravado, were they thinking something the same thing too?

After dinner, we proceeded to the bar for one more drink, as we were all too excited to go to sleep at 8:30. I left them there at about 9 pm and headed back to get organized for the morning. I decided it was NOT a good idea to start my Camino feeling tired.

I was still awake, though, when they came back from the bar, and the lights were already off in the dorm. The Dutch girl was supporting the Dutch guy and helped him into a bottom bunk near me. He was going to be feeling a bit tired in the morning!

I stuck my head back under my sleeping bag to finish a bit of blogging on my phone. I had decided to blog about the trip, so people would not worry about me and they could track my progress every day. It would also give me something to do when I had finished walking for the day.

I hadn't considered how hard it would be to type on my phone and upload photos with lousy Wi-Fi, though. I also hadn't considered how lucky it was that I had brought two phone chargers with me. Somehow, I left one behind the next morning. Maybe it even made it to the chuck-it-or-pluck-it table too!

2

WITCH WAY?

DAY 2-RONCESVALLES TO ZUBIRI-22 KM

"Truth itself wanders through the forest." - Werner Herzog

A little after 6 am, the lights flickered on. People groaned, yawned, and swore. One of the mighty monastic male volunteers walked through the dorm smiling (maliciously?) strumming on a guitar, and singing, "Good morning! Hello! El Camino is waiting for you!"

Nobody was enthused with this early morning wake-up

call, myself included. But people began to stir, and I figured that I should too.

I saw that the Italian father and son duo seemed to have coordinated brief underwear as they stood digging in their packs. It seemed they had not had a shower the night before, nor were they planning to now. The manly smell of L'eau de Camino was also a good wake-up call for me. That pungent smell of B.O. took my breath away in the way that the mountain views had not yet.

I grabbed a quick breakfast at the small restaurant by myself. Just some coffee and toast and jam, and then I was off, following the shapes of other backpacks moving in the misty darkness ahead of me.

I had wanted to start this day by myself, so I left early and knew I'd see Lina later. Someone took a photo of me in front of a famous mileage sign just outside the monastery, which read 790 kilometers to Santiago. After that, everything suddenly seemed very real, and there was no turning back.

I got into a good rhythm with my poles and soon caught up to a fun group of five Italian guys. I walked with them for a while. They were all students and were walking to Santiago too. Eventually, they walked on ahead, a little faster than me, and I focused on my steps.

"Buen Camino!" we said to each other, and we knew we'd see each other later in the day.

Remember the film *The Blair Witch Project* with the thickly wooded areas, dead leafless trees, rotting leaves, and no sounds? I'm pretty sure they filmed it on this bit of the Camino. It was the perfect setting for a mystery movie; kind of dark, lush, and very quiet. I expected at any time for something to jump out at me as I walked on alone. The problem was the silence, the lack of wind, and the darkness in the heavy forest. Where had those crazy Italians suddenly gone who had just been wishing me a "Buen Camino?" They had better not be planning on jumping out from behind a tree!

Suddenly it got even worse; I heard a crack of a branch. Most of the forest was comprised of big gnarled beech trees with moss creeping up from the bottom. I knew the sound I had heard was just a dead branch falling, but there was no reaction from the forest. No birds, no movement, and a gentle rain continued. I knew I was paranoid, but it was just so freaking still. I kept thinking about that philosophical rant, "If a tree falls in a forest, and no one is around to hear it, does it make a sound?"

And then there was that iconic line from *Alien* too. "In space, nobody can hear you scream." Would somebody hear me scream in that forest?

I think what set off these thoughts was the blurb I had read in the guidebook. A secret witch coven had once inhabited this forest area near Burguete, where I was now walking. Witches had even been burnt at the stake in the main square. (This information hadn't been included in my pre-Camino party pack!)

Lots of these thoughts were going through my head, and I was soon thankful to meet the Italian guys again, who had been resting a little ahead.

"It's so quiet in here," I said to them.

"Yes, you can hear your thinking. It is like, how you say, a time warp?"

I loved how that was translated to English; I wondered what the words were in Italian. However, it did make me think a bit of the *Rocky Horror Picture Show*, and that just scared me more!

We walked and talked through the Sorginaritzaga Forest, "Oak Grove of Witches."

Some of the most well-known witch trials of the 16th century were held near here, and nine women were burned at the stake for practicing witchcraft. These women would collect plants and use them as a natural medicine to help others. This was their only crime.

It felt otherworldly and sad in that forest, with the dappled light filtering through the trees. Yet, despite my thoughts, the walk was wonderful. Within a couple of kilometers, we emerged to see some buildings ahead, where there was also a cross and an information sign. The sign detailed the history of this 16th-century wood as a favorite meeting place for the local witches' coven. A white Cross had been placed there as a reminder.

It was a beautiful forest, really, and probably had been good for harvesting medicinal herbs. Witches had been the pharmacists of the 16th century but hadn't got off well. They definitely would have known how to help with blisters!

This harassment of women and children is a bit of a dark side to the Camino de Santiago. Witches should be treated as symbols of female wisdom. They were early scientists, doctors, botanists, and pharmacists. No doubt their thinking scared everyone back then.

The word 'pharmakeia' originally meant "Magic, sorcery, witchcraft; and was often found in connection with idolatry." Farmacias in Spain have come a long way.

The Italians had walked on ahead, and I was walking alone with my creepy thoughts when I met an odd hippie sitting on the ground in front of a shop in the first town I came through: Burguete.

I was planning to enter the shop, but he reached up his hand and said, "Here, eat this orange." I took it quickly because he seemed like a person I didn't want to piss off.

He reminded me of both Charles Manson and Russell Brand. Yes, just imagine that for a second! Dread-locks, well-worn jeans, and a tattered t-shirt with some rock band logo and lots of silver rings on his dirty fingers. He also had bright, bulging, crazy eyes, and it seemed like it would take nothing to make him snap.

"Too many people on this path. They follow each other like sheep. I don't like sheep, and I don't like people," he moaned to me as I took off my bag, eased myself into a sitting position beside him, and concentrated on peeling my small orange.

I had hardly seen a soul except for the Italians, but I just mumbled, "Mmm, hmmm," hoping to avoid much conversation.

"I am Peter. I am from Amsterdam." He offered me a hand.

"I'm Shannon, from Canada," shaking his sticky hand and trying not to grimace.

"Mmm," now was his only reply.

He reached out then and grabbed the orange, peeled it for me, and then handed it back, carefully putting the orange peels in a side pocket of his bag. Good, I had wondered what to do with those. Apparently, I was too slow.

"I'm going to cut to another path, to the Camino Norte, to get some peace," he continued in his guttural Dutch accent as he sat sucking slowly on pieces of his own orange with dirty fingernails. Some of the juice ran down his chin, and he flicked his snake-like tongue around to clean up any escaping drops.

With breakfast done, he now moved on to caring for his feet. He carefully unlaced some well-worn leather boots and pulled them off to reveal blackened and blood-stained whitish Sports socks.

Please, please do not pull off your socks, I thought to myself. Please... but of course he did.

Off came one sock, then the other, and I tried not to gasp as I saw the extent of his raw, bleeding blisters on the back of his heels. The blistered skin had all peeled off, and now another reddened layer was exposed like my once-half peeled orange.

I began eating the orange as fast as possible, almost choking on the small pieces, trying to avoid looking at his painful heels, but of course, I could not.

"Those look painful. I have some Compeed (special blister band-aids) if you want."

He turned and stared at me. He looked a little angry.

"Compeed are for tourists," he snarled. "I use the Dutch method," and pulled a dirty joint out of his jeans, sparked it up, took a long drag, and offered it to me.

I thought about it, but the orange juice nestled in the side of his lips, his crazy eyes, and those dirty fingers put me off just a bit.

"No thanks," I said, not really wanting to experience my second day on the Camino paranoid in the middle of nowhere.

He just shrugged and killed off the joint with long, annoying drags and occasional coughing fits.

With now slightly reddened, less wild eyes, he turned his attention back to his feet, which had been enjoying the gentle morning breeze. He dug in this pack and pulled out some socks that seemed a little cleaner than the other pair.

"Ok, I will try some Compeed now," he said.

It was truly amazing what the effects of a good joint could do.

I passed some Compeed over, and he peeled them and stuck them on top of the blisters, pulled on the new socks, laced up his boots, and got ready to leave.

His backpack was huge; a sleeping bag, tent, cooking pots, and water bottles dangled from it.

"I started in Le Puy, and I always camped. Very peaceful. Few people."

He desired solitude while I wanted community.

He reached out his hand and gave me another small orange, stood up, and struggled with his pack a bit.

"Stupid Camino!" he said as he finally got his pack adjusted and gave me a wave before he headed off with his pots clinking.

I smiled and watched him walk ahead. Would I see him

again? Did I mention his crazy eyes? I had to laugh because my Camino greeting from him seemed pretty apt.

I dribbled some water on my sticky fingers and headed off too. There were only a few other pilgrims around as I passed through the rest of the small town.

Burguete was a beautiful medieval town of stone houses with red and green shutters and many Camino markers showing which way to go. Or was it "witch" way? Ernest Hemingway vacationed here and mentioned the village in his novel, *The Sun Also Rises.*

It resembled a Swiss village with balconies overflowing with red geraniums and perfect cobblestoned streets. Little canals flowed beside the sidewalks. Outside the Hostal Burguete was a large panel with a picture of Hemingway. If truth be told, it reminded me of the scene from Beauty and the Beast, a quaint village but without the people. It was mostly deserted when I passed through.

Instead of Belle saying "Bonjour" in a poor provincial town, there were just a few other pilgrims and me saying "Buen Camino." Imagine if you lived here and had an army of pilgrims trudging through town early every morning, still clean, fresh, and excited and just starting their Camino.

Sometime later, walking through another enchanted forest of what looked like beech trees, I caught up to a smiling grey-haired woman struggling a bit and pausing for breath often. She had a small staff and a little white bag, and her backpack.

There were a lot of uphill bits here and loose gravel as well. It wasn't lost on me that I found a person alone in a forest where a bunch of witches once hung out.

But, I was so happy to meet someone.

"This is a crazy hard day, eh?" I said to her as I paused for breath beside her. Sometimes I sounded so Canadian.

"Em, How are you? It's a bit tough here, alright," she replied.

23

Ah, she was Irish. Interesting. We began to walk together and found out a bit about each other.

Her name was Maeve, and she was from a little coastal town in Ireland past Cork. She didn't easily share information about herself, but I pieced a few things together. Her husband had been a doctor, and she was a nurse. They worked together in Africa somewhere for many years, but he'd passed away several years ago. Her son had done the Camino last year and urged her to do it as well.

She'd traveled a lot and complained of all the trinkets from little countries that she had collected, like rugs and blankets and wall art. (This sounded a lot like me too!) She had packed them all up and sealed them away in boxes.

"I'm no longer looking back at my life," she shared, quite matter-of-factly. "I'm at a point where I don't need reminding about where I've been or what I've done! I might just throw it all in the tip one day. It's just all collecting dust, and my house is too small!"

"I wish I could do that too!" I said.

She was a jewel of a woman, and I'm so glad to have met her.

We walked together and kept finding out little bits about each other. We shared some chocolate and nuts, and the talking helped us forget about the steepness, the hazardous rocks on high ledges, and the loose rocks going down steep hills. I was a bit surprised by how dangerous it was in points.

Maeve was in her late 60s, and she walked like she was in her 20s. She told me she walked a good ten miles a day on her property up a few hills, and I have no doubt she was more fit than I was.

If we didn't concentrate on each step, there was a good chance of going ass over tits off the side of the mountain. The track was also slippery from the recent rain, and it was hard on the knees. Luckily, mine were in good shape, but I thought of the South Africa woman from the dorm in St Jean and wondered how she would do on this section.

Somewhere while we sat having a snack, Lina caught up to us. I was thrilled to see her again. Two young German girls, Anna and Laura, also began to walk with us, so then there were 5 of us.

We were all very, very tired when we got to Zubiri and checked into the first albergue on the main street into town overlooking the river. I looked out the window of our small six-bunk dorm room and saw the young Danish couple from Roncesvalles putting their aching feet in the river. They couldn't hold them in for too long; the water was too cold. My feet were aching too, but I couldn't be bothered to walk down to the river. I'd never had aching feet before; a mouthful of Tylenol helped a lot, as did some beer.

The German girls were only 18. One of them was about to take a government job for life. The other was an Education student. They were both really sweet, and I wondered how they felt about sharing a room with Lina, Maeve, and me. We were quite a bit older than them. It's weird, but the 5 of us were up late giggling like it was a sleep-over. I loved the Camino already!

Zubiri meant "the village of the bridge" in the Basque language. The medieval stone bridge we walked over dated back to the 12th century and was known as the Puente de la Rabia. The English translation meant Bridge of Rabies.

According to the history, animals that passed under the bridge's arches three times would be miraculously healed of any illness (including rabies!). I'm not sure how factual the folklore was but, I could see how the refreshing water lured peregrinos to enter and relax. No rabid animal sightings from our window look-out as far as I could tell.

The owner of the albergue washed and dried my clothes for a few euros, and the shower was nice and hot. Then, feeling refreshed, we all headed out for dinner, and I was happy to see Marie there, too.

It was a pizza and beer night at the Cafe del Camino, and already everyone felt like old friends. This place was the only show in town, and our large group of Hansel and Gretel (my nicknames for the Dutch couple whose names I have forgotten), Maria (Wonder woman), Lina, Maeve, Laura, and Anna shared some thoughts on the Dutch hippy who Maria and the Dutch couple had also met. The consensus was don't look too deeply into his eyes and watch out for poisoned apples or oranges!

Everyone already had blisters and sore feet. Our shared discussion of pain seemed to be playing a significant role in our formation of solidarity. Usually, back in our countries, we did not depend on our bodies or our feet so much with our various jobs. Even though we all wore relatively expensive shoes or boots, it was our feet that were important. They were going to get us to Santiago, hopefully. And even though we were all going through physically demanding days, we did all seem to have a lot of energy and strength. The beer and pizza probably helped a lot!

These new companions were like my first mirror on the Camino; I saw a bit of myself in everyone's face that I looked at. I didn't like what I saw in everyone. I had 32 days not to be so judgmental, to give people more time to talk, and to listen to the words of Aaron Burr from Hamilton, "Listen more, and talk less!"

3

THE SUN SETS AND ALSO RISES

DAY 3-ZUBIRI TO PAMPLONA -21 KM

"It is good to have an end to journey toward; but it is the journey that matters in the end." – Ernest Hemingway

. . .

We got an early start again this day, at around 7 am. Saran-wrapped plates of bread, cheese, and meat were laid out at a long table with about ten settings. There were also carafes of coffee and orange juice on the table. We gulped things down, then grabbed our bags, and our shoes from the shoebox, and we were off once more.

I was extremely excited to be walking towards Pamplona, the city of bulls, tapas, and probably many pilgrims. In July, The Festival of San Fermin, widely known as the Running of the Bulls, is held here. Men and sometimes women run through the narrow streets trying to avoid being gored by the bulls that are chasing them. It is a tangible display of 'machismo'—the ultimate thrill of being close to a raging bull and possible death. It was about as close to being a bullfighter as you could get.

Ernest Hemingway set his novel *The Sun Also Rises* about the doomed love affair between Jake and Brett here and really put Pamplona and the bullfights on the map for many people. But, as Jake said, "Nobody ever lives their life all the way up except bullfighters."

I was thinking of doing a Hemingway reality food, drink, and think tour in Pamplona (I didn't see any on offer, though). Probably these would have been too unprofitable as they would have involved consuming huge Hemingway amounts of tapas and wine, followed by discussions and prose writing on fishing and bull-fighting. An evening of soak-up-all-the-booze with chocolate churros at one of his old hangouts, Cafe Irun, would have been a nice final touch. Papa Hem was lucky he lived in the century he did since all that machismo would not have come off well in our woke Me-Too days, that is for sure.

Most of the morning, the walk into Pamplona followed a path beside the River Agra, which went up and down through quaint towns of stone buildings and stoic-looking people. We eventually got to the Magdalene Bridge, the gateway into Pamplona. Pamplona had a population of about 200,000.

Finally, after three days of rural walking, it was a chance to walk into the streets of a bustling city.

We had our first experience of following the Camino markers along the sidewalks and across busy streets here. We found that in Pamplona, the local people were used to seeing pilgrims and could be asked directions if we looked like we were lost. But, unfortunately, it didn't always go well.

"Donde esta Cafe Irun?" someone in our little group tried when we were lost in a downtown traffic maze in the afternoon.

Several people launched into rapid-fire Spanish, looked at us angrily, and pointed in various directions. Not too helpful, but at least they tried.

The city Camino signs were not as well-marked as those in the countryside. But we had phones, so if we really seemed off the track, we had a look at Google maps.

The last 4 km into Pamplona was residential, which felt odd and a bit eerie since everything was shut down from 2 pm to 5 pm. It seemed to take an awfully long time to got to the albergue as it was past car dealers and small shops and then busy downtown streets where it was so hard to see yellow arrows. The last bit was finally up the hill into an old medieval part of town.

There were massive stone walls that once guarded the city. We climbed the old road into the city and crossed a working medieval drawbridge that was still raised and lowered once a year. Finally.

We stayed in the old town at the Jesus and Mary hostel. This was a huge albergue in an old building with hundreds of beds in large, open rooms. The building had once been a church, and walls had been built in alcoves to give it a unique shape. It still had the marvelous acoustics that you'd expect a church to have. Too bad snoring was the only music these days!

Once settled in, I sat on my top bunk, examining my blisters, which had now appeared on the balls of both feet and the back heel. Could it be that my delicate feet were just not used to the distance? I poked them a bit and then just decided what the heck and quickly plunged the needle into the watery blisters on my soles.

It was a little messy. For added good measure, I smeared a little antiseptic on my soles like I was buttering a piece of toast badly. This blister popping seemed like the right medical thing to do. I was sure I must have seen that on Grey's Anatomy once, too.

Soon, I enrolled in the Blisters for Beginners class taught by Lina and Maeve (one was a nurse; the other sold medical equipment, which made them infinitely more experienced than me!).

They had a good, long look at my feet as I dangled them off my top bunk.

They barely flinched.

"You've got to put some thread through those. That will drain the liquid out," Maeve suggested.

"Yes, it is the best thing," Lina concurred.

"OK, I'll try that later," I lied.

I was not too fond of the sound of the needle and thread method, and I'd already let the fluid out, so I didn't bother to listen to them—cue ominous music. The blister on my heel, I decided to completely ignore.

I had a pretty crappy first aid kit with me. There were a few Band-Aids, one needle, a tube of antiseptic, and a chapstick. I'd heard of people eating chapstick when their supply of food ran out. I hoped it would never come to that, as the flavor was Vanilla Mint.

"Have you had any problems with blisters yet?" I asked Lina.

"No, but I lubricate my feet every day before walking. I think it helps."

"Maybe I'll try that." My blisters seemed to be getting worse, but I was trying to ignore them.

I hobbled down to the shower, this time co-ed, and I took my clothes into the shower stall with me. Unfortunately, the clean ones fell off the hook on the door and into the water, so now I had wet clean clothes as opposed to dry dirty ones. I'm not sure which was better. And why did I even bother, because the Europeans walked around with nothing on anyhow!

A bit later, I went into town with the others. So many restaurants were packed with people enjoying the night around a central square, including the Café Irun. It was dark and smokey when I peaked my head in, and we had a coffee at the outdoor tables in front, imagining Hemingway sitting there and Jake and Brett hanging out with the expatriate bohemians.

It did not possess the torpid debauchery of Hemingway's youth (mostly excited teenagers sat checking their phones, not speaking to one another), nor did it offer the best churros, but the coffee was good, as was the elegant architecture. Lots of families seemed to be inside, enjoying the ambiance at least.

There was a wine festival going on outside, and people were standing around the streets drinking, smoking, and passing out. Outside many bars were old wine barrels that served as tables for people standing around drinking and smoking. We settled for some pintxos and wine ourselves at Bar Gaucho but didn't get to the passing-out stage. We elbowed our way past the other patrons and ordered at the bar. We were practically locals.

The Burger King near the church and our albergue was doing a brisk business with drunk Spaniards walking in for a Whopper to go along with all that alcohol. Hemingway would have been proud, I am sure.

The others went back to the dorms, and I stopped at a Farmacia to purchase some Compeed Glide. I wanted to lube up my feet a bit and hopefully prevent a lot of the friction that was causing the blisters.

Already I loved the little Spanish pharmacies identified by the green cross outside, sometimes illuminated and visible as a lighthouse on a stormy night. They were not large, and inside was an organized battalion of supplies for those on the pilgrim battle with blisters or other ailments. Common items like painkillers had to be asked for behind the counter. There were no extra strength bottles with hundreds of pills inside that you could just grab off the shelf like in the U.S.

I had a bit of a headache, so I thought it would be a good time to stock up my first-aid kit. I realized, though, that I didn't know the Spanish word for headache. I was a moron!

"Ow," I tried holding my head and looking sad. I have been an ESL teacher for many years and knew the importance of good acting, haha!

But darn, I also thought. My hours of learning Spanish on Babel were helpful for short conversations, and, yes, I now had a good grasp of basic restaurant and hotel Spanish. But, my Spanish illness vocabulary was non-existent, so I'd have to go back and put in my earbuds and listen to those words later. No doubt, it would be useful to know at least the Spanish word for blisters too. That way, I wouldn't have to thrust my ankle up on the counter if things got worse!

The pharmacist had a stony-faced reaction to my "Ow" but reached into a long brown drawer and pulled out a small box of ibuprofen; twelve 400 mg tablets.

"Take one every 6 hours. Do not take more than three a day," she said in perfect punctuated, possibly pissed-off English.

"Oh, OK, thanks," I said, embarrassed by my over-acting.

"And, do you have any Compeed Glide or something like it? Something to prevent blisters?" I wasn't even going to attempt any more Spanish.

Again, she reached into a drawer and pulled out another prize; it was smaller than an airport size deodorant. I received a green tube of Compeed Glide, which I could rub onto my feet.

"Thanks so much, um, gracias," I added somewhat pathetically as I handed over some euros and received my change.

She smiled then and said quietly, "Buen Camino." She was about 40 years old, wearing a white blouse, no make-up, and had medium-length hair. I could see a room behind her where another man counted pills. I noticed then she looked tired. How many countless pilgrims had asked her for ibuprofen and something for blisters? That smile meant so much to me.

I had tried smearing Vaseline on my feet back home during some long practice walks. It had just made my socks gooey, and I never had blisters then, anyway. Perhaps the Glide would help, but it seemed like it was already too late. Anyhow, I would try it in the morning.

It was an experience staying at the Pamplona albergue; it was only 10 euros a night, but I didn't get much sleep as a super-snorer was near me. Unfortunately, the wax earplugs I'd purchased for such an occasion didn't block out all the noise. And, the snoring was at a volume that I hadn't even imagined was possible.

Fortunately, I was exhausted from the walking and fell asleep, but later was woken by people shouting, bunks creaking, and then at 5 a.m., people rustling around in their bags. The sun also rises whether you are tired or not!

4

MEETING ANGELINA

DAY 4 - PAMPLONA TO PUENTE LA REINA -24KM

"Walking is good for solving problems — it's like the feet are little psychiatrists." — Pepper Giardino

. . .

We 'glided' out from Pamplona early, and, yes, my feet were smeared with the my new walking lubricant. I was hoping for a miracle, but not holding my breath. Perhaps I should have been though, since the heavy yeasty smells of beer and sickly sweet morning smells of wine were still in the air.

The streets had the remnants of the previous night's wine festival. Broken glass and plastic cups were littered everywhere. We even passed a few people who had not made it home from the night before. Already yellow-vested workers were cleaning up the debris and spraying the streets with powerful blasts of cleansing water.

And so began another day of walking. There were small towns to pass through and coffee and lemonade were sold from vans or at small stands all day. Usually, there was a town about every 5 km where you could have a coffee and use the toilet. The towns were still gorgeous, medieval-style villages with thick stone buildings and cobblestone streets. They were visible in the distance, and they always seemed to be at the top of a damn hill! A church was always at the center of a town, and a cafe was close by. Often, there was a small shop to purchase fruit, snacks, and odds and ends, too.

Today was a walk to Alto del Perdon (The Peak of Forgiveness), and it commemorated all the pilgrims who have walked this way over the years. It was a strenuous walk up here, and everyone deserved a medal, but a sculpture would have to do.

Massive modern white wind turbines sat in the distance on the ridge like watchful statues, and we heard them whirring loudly as we got closer. They sliced the air, cutting through silence and making new mournful sounds.

It was a beautiful view from the top of Mount Perdon, looking down below at where we had started from. The metal Peregrino monument from the movie *The Way* was now a famous identifiable landmark for many, and everyone took photos of themselves doing a poised Peregrino pose before almost being blown off the cliff.

An inscription here read:

"Donde se cruzado el camino del vent con el de las
   estrellas." The English translation -*Where the path of*
   the wind crosses with the stars.

According to one famous Camino legend, a medieval pilgrim climbing this ridge was dying of exhaustion and thirst. The devil showed up, dressed as a pilgrim, and promised to reveal the location of a water spring if the pilgrim would renounce God. The exhausted pilgrim refused multiple times. Miraculously, an apostle appeared and insisted that the devil provide the pilgrim with water. The location of a spring was revealed to the pilgrim near the summit. But what happened to the Devil and the Apostle?

I didn't see a spring up top this time. However, a guy was selling drinks and snacks out of a small van, and we sat on the rocks for a while, glad that the walk up was over. He had cans of Coke and cookies for sale on cardboard tables he had set up outside.

I took some bottled water and cookies back to Lina, Maeve, and the German girls.

"I read about that guy in my German guidebook," said Lina. "He will drive pilgrims to the next town if they are too tired to walk. It's nice and necessary for some people, I think."

We all nodded together, feeling thankful that we had made it to the top and for the non-spring bottled water. We were all hoping that we wouldn't need a ride in the van later. It was good to have options though.

We could see 3 or 4 towns stretched out into the distance

like charms on a bracelet from the top. They looked a long, long way off.

The walk down toward Puente La Reina was almost worse than going up. In the Brierley guide, the elevation changes were also marked. Thus, you could see how far up and down you may need to walk.

I was already ignoring the elevation profiles in the book. I didn't want to know! The walk down was very steep and eroded, and wooden planks had been put in some spots to stop the hill from completely collapsing. My knees were pretty happy to get into the town below. I was so glad to have the poles for balance.

As we walked through more small towns, the atmosphere was eerie. They seemed absolutely deserted, with shutters closed and shops not open. A few dogs were lying around, but we saw few people, children playing, or cars as we walked through.

"Where is everyone? These are like ghost towns."

"People have moved to the cities for work. They might come back for holiday times. I think there is not enough business for them here now."

In one town, we found a shop and a small bar open. Pilgrims were sitting around savoring beer and examining blisters. It already seemed like perfectly normal behavior.

We got a fantastic hostel in Puente La Reina with a sliding door to a small patio and washed some clothes in machines and hung them out. The vending machine outside our room here had everything from bandaids to beer. It was like our own personal little convenience store with Compeed, antiseptic, pregnancy tests, USB cables, Cup Noodles, and lots of chocolate bars and snacks. Who needed to go out?

I couldn't believe all the Korean people walking on this day. There were small families, retired friends, students, and solo travelers. Apparently, there was a popular documentary on this route, and it caused a boom among Koreans coming to do the Camino.

I'd met one Japanese guy, lots of Germans, Italians, Irish, Dutch, and a handful of Canadians and Americans. People were indeed from all over the world here.

I'd already noticed people felt safe sharing personal stories and deep feelings with each other. Perhaps it was because we had no connection to each other, and we might never meet again. Yet, all day people offered each other encouragement and listened, I think, with little judgment. We were all on the same path, headed the same place, and all walking in the same direction. We only had each other.

Someone told me that they had cancer, another person mentioned that they had been in a horrific car accident and had learned to walk again. There were so many stories and so many reasons for being there.

A Brazilian lady shared a bunk in our room that night and said that she had been wandering the globe, living out of her backpack for many years. She was only about 5 feet tall, with long, coarse, black hair now streaked with grey. Her face was weather-worn and wrinkled, but her dancing green eyes and a warm smile lit up our room. I guessed she was in her 60s, and she must have been stunning in her youth. She wore a faded Levi's jacket, dusty black pants, and her ears and arms were weighed down with silver earrings and bracelets. Peregrinos did not dress like her. We had to carry light washable clothing. She was dressed as if she was going out bar-hopping in the evening.

Her name was Angelina.

"Let's go out for pintxos and some wine," she said after we had all settled in and introduced ourselves. The two German girls were staying in another dorm room and decided to stay back, so it was just Lina, Maeve, Angelina, and me for dinner.

We had a delicious pilgrim's meal out on the main square

(We all helped pay for Angelina's dinner, as she was a little short of cash. Was she scamming us or not?)

She was definitely a bit unusual, but we had no reason not to believe her stories, and we enjoyed a lovely meal in a square where families gathered with kids riding on bikes. The food wasn't great; you knew you were a pilgrim when you ate a salad, dry bread, and rubbery chicken and wanted more!

This night was my first real pilgrim's meal. The previous three nights, I had just ordered off a menu. A pilgrim's meal always gave you a choice of an appetizer; either a mixed salad, a soup, or spaghetti. The main course was a choice of meat with french fries. Bring on the carbs. Dessert was ice cream or flan. A carafe of wine was usually included too. Wow! For 10 euros a night, maybe I could be like Angelina and live out of my backpack for years?

"How long have you been on the Camino?" I asked her.

"It has been many years. I think 5. Sometimes I volunteer at an albergue for a while. I was working at Hospital de Orbigo last. You must go there. It is a magical place." I decided to try to remember this. I loved how she spoke without contractions. It seemed like English of long ago somehow.

"And why do you keep walking the Camino?" I asked.

"It is the reason we all walk it."

"What's that?"

"The Camino is our mother. Mother Earth. We are going to be nurtured, to grow, and to go through the stages of our life again."

"May I have more wine, please?" Angelina asked.

"Em," said Maeve. "I am not looking for any mother you can be sure. I am here to follow my heart and to be near Our Lord."

"Yes," Angelina said. "But, Mother Earth is our god and goddess. The Camino can awaken the spirit within us. A little more wine, I think, please."

"I'm walking the Camino to be more fit and disconnect from work and see a little more of Spain," said Lina. I'm pretty confident that she was trying to referee between a developing Maeve versus Angelina argument.

"Mmm," said Angelina.

"I am just walking to see if I can do it," I said, also trying to keep things in the conversation smooth.

"Mmmm," said Angelina. "You may find it is a bit more than a walk."

We talked some more. Maeve was fuming. She had a very strong Catholic faith and likely did not appreciate Angelina's thoughts. She didn't speak to her anymore and soon excused herself and went back to the room.

Lina and I sat talking with Angelina for a while longer.

"Have you really been living out of a backpack for five years?"

"Yes, I have traveled everywhere that I have wanted to go. I have had many loves, many jobs, and many heartbreaks. I have four children who are grown and barely speak to me. I was never enough of a mother to them. I suppose that is why I have been drawn to the Camino. It nurtures me when I could not nurture them. Shall we have some more wine?"

"Not for me," I said.

"Me, neither," said Lina. "We will start early tomorrow."

"Ok, then I will sit here a little longer tonight. Thank you for the company. Buen Camino."

Maeve was already asleep when we got back. So I climbed up onto the creaky upper metal bunk and fell asleep immediately.

5

THE THINGS WE CARRIED

DAY 5- PUENTE LA REINA TO ESTELLA-22 KM

"It's your road and yours alone. Others may walk it with you, but no one can walk it for you."- Rumi

We woke to the sound of a 6 am alarm. As we were packing up the bags, I glanced over at Angelina's bunk. It was empty; she had not come back. Her sleeping bag lay neatly on the bottom bunk across from me.

Her backpack was open, and some old clothes spilled out. A notebook, a towel, and a bottle of something were all visible.

"Do you think Angelina is ok? She didn't come back last night," I asked Lina and Maeve.

"That's one I wouldn't worry about. She knows exactly what she is doing," Maeve said. It seemed like her lips were even slightly turned up with disdain. What was that all about?

The morning started with very heavy rain, and we sat in the hotel's common area for a while, drinking coffee and waiting for it to stop. When it let up a bit about an hour later, we donned our rain jackets and decided to walk for a while and stop for a coffee and breakfast at the first town we came to.

The arrows guided us past the main square where we had been sitting at night. I half-expected Angelina to be sleeping at a table, but she was nowhere in sight.

I wondered if Angelina had stayed away because of Maeve. The energy between them had not been good. They were both too similar. Maeve was a survivor, and I suspected her strong Catholic faith had got her through many hardships in life.

Angelina had survived on her wits and her spirituality. She was warm and open and made friends easily. Yet, there was underlying desperation and sadness there. I would have liked to have got to know her a bit better. Maybe we would meet again someplace.

The three of us walked out of Puente La Reina, saying little.

The bridge in this town translated to 'Bridge of the Queen' and was from the 11th century. We had to walk over it to get out of town. It was a pedestrian-only bridge with Roman arches, and it looked brilliant and otherworldly in the morning light and gentle rain.

The wife of Sancho III commissioned the bridge to help medieval pilgrims cross the river on their way to Santiago. It was hard to walk over a bridge that had been there for a thousand years without wondering about all the remarkable stories of the millions of pilgrims who had walked across the same stone path over the centuries.

We kept walking uphill and eventually came to the beautiful medieval-style village of Ciraqui, where everyone seemed to have stopped for lunch.

There was only one thing on the menu at the cafe; lentil soup. It was served in large metal tureens that were brought steaming hot to the tables. You just sat wherever there was an empty chair and helped yourself. Plates loaded with pieces of bread were carried out too.

We ended up sharing a table with a couple of British women who had decided to call it quits. They didn't like the albergues, the food, or this 'too simple' homemade lentil soup. They were taking a taxi back to Pamplona and then planned on going up north to San Sebastian and laying on the beach for a while.

"This pilgrim life is not for me," one woman said. "I am looking forward to a beach, a comfy bed, and a big pitcher of Sangria!"

Although that did sound good, too, I loved the walking and the experience. We were now walking through farming towns, vineyards, and olive orchards. The landscape was constantly changing.

We walked a lot of the day on old Roman roads, medieval bridges, and country roads. We met the German girls in a town we past through. Laura had twisted her ankle walking down a hill, and the girls were sitting on the street waiting for an albergue to open. They were both close to tears, but they were also two very brave and determined young ladies. I had no doubt that they would make it to Santiago.

We ended up this evening at a lovely place in Estella called Albergue Capuchinos. It was spotless, in a good location, and had a private bathroom with a great hot shower. It was working out well for Lina, Maeve, and me to share a room. We had a bit more privacy than in large dorm rooms.

The albergue was managed by the Catholic order of Capuchinos brothers, who had a long history with Saint James (Santiago) and the Camino. Nowadays, they provided support and religious guidance to the pilgrim community in Spain.

The dormitory was attached to an old church, and the modern, clean bunk rooms lined a renovated hall with centuries-old antiques. Crosses, antique chairs, old photos, clean wooden floors, and whitewashed walls made you feel like you were in a very safe, welcoming environment. Did I mention they provided real sheets, a big blanket, and a cover to each pilgrim?

Estella was a quaint little town with some interesting points of interest (according to the guidebook), but we were too tired to go sightseeing. So after a hot shower and a handful of Tylenol, I limped down the stairs for dinner. A husband and wife were the only other patrons, and they were cycling section of the Camino.

"How is the cycling going?"

"There are a lot of steep sections where we have to push our bikes up, but the downhill is worth it." Not too dissimilar to the walking experience, but just a bit faster, I thought.

The albergue had a great custard dessert I will never forget! It was a traditional dessert called 'Natillas,' a delicious custard topped with cinnamon and a Sweet Marie cookie. Absolute bliss.

Fortunately, we were very close to Decathlon (a Spanish sporting goods shop), where I bought some cheap running shoes after dinner. My hiking shoes, which I had worn for months already, were evil things I'd decided. They were giving me severe blisters, despite the Glide additions. I also bought one more t-shirt to wear, since I had already forgotten one someplace. I seemed to be leaving pieces of myself all over Spain!

It was strange to be in a store as the outside world now seemed so distant. Even the TVs that were always turned on inside the bars we entered for a coffee played news that seemed far away. Those daytime cafe con leches always tasted so good, and there was never any rush to finish it or a necessity to watch the news. Life had already taken on a different pace and a different sense of time.

I hoped my Decathlon purchases would not make much difference in the weight of my pack. I was reminded of the book, *The Things They Carried,* by Tim O'Brien. It was amazing what the different soldiers had in their bags and what was important to them; pictures of home, bags of marijuana, ponchos, good luck charms, and even pebbles.

I carried things that were important to me, too. But, of course, my phone, my Camino guidebook, and my extra shoes were the most important. The many things I carried were each important in their own way, and everything was necessary to get me to my goal of Santiago. Well, maybe not the copy of *On the Road* that I was now regretting.

As we organized our bunks to go to sleep, I asked Maeve and Lina if they carried any luxury items in their backpacks.

Lina told me she carried a good-sized pocket knife. She

had walked the Camino before from Astorga and had been followed on a lonely stretch of the Camino.

There had once been a terrible tragedy on that section of the Camino where a pilgrim named Denise Thiem was sadly murdered.

"I don't know if I could ever use this little knife," Lina said. "It just makes me feel a little safer."

I had also purchased a little Swiss army type knife in St Jean too; mostly for the corkscrew attachment! I wasn't worried, I knew that the Camino was a very, very safe walk.

"Em, I have an embroidered pillowcase cover," said Maeve. "I embroidered it myself, and it has an Irish blessing on it." She showed it to me, and I smiled. I had always loved that little poem but hadn't noticed it on her pillowcase.

"May the road rise up to meet you.
May the wind be always at your back.
May the sun shine warm upon your face;
The rains fall soft upon your fields,
and until we meet again,
May God hold you in the palm of His hand."

I knew that she put her own pillowcase over any pillow we had in an albergue; it must have made her feel at home. She also had a pair of pajamas that she wore most nights. Her pack was full of comfortable touches.

6

OF WINE AND RABBITS

DAY 6- ESTELLA TO LOS ARCOS-22 KM

"The secret of getting ahead is getting started." – Mark Twain

We arrived in Los Arcos around 4 pm and managed to get the last three beds after a long day of walking. It was April, not the busiest month, but there was still a race for a bed? In the busy summer months on the Camino, I knew it was necessary to leave early or walk quickly to get to some smaller towns first where there might be a limitation on accommodations. I hadn't pre-booked any nights anywhere because I wanted the freedom to decide how far to walk each day. It seemed we had been fortunate in Los Arcos, however, on this day.

The fun part of the day had been in the early morning at a place called Bodegas Irache, a winery where 100 liters of wine are dispensed per day at a fountain for all of those who walk by.

There was a sign saying that: *"this stretch of the Way to Compostela was already renowned for the quality of the local wine in the 12th century, and the Calixtine Codex mentions Estella, land of Good Bread and Optimal Wine."*

I came prepared with my scallop shell. Perhaps it wasn't noon yet, but it was Happy Hour somewhere! It was definitely morning Wine Time in Spain!

I don't know what I expected, maybe something like an elaborate Willy Wonka chocolate fountain that dispensed wine instead. This wine fountain was just a tap with a webcam above; it was supposed to track overly thirsty pilgrims. It was good marketing for the wineries, that was for sure.

I had a sip of wine out of the shell; did I detect oak and a hint of chocolate in my wine tasting? I couldn't be sure, but it was a nice smooth Rioja anyway you swallowed it! Some pilgrim connoisseurs were filling up plastic bottles, but I thought I would stick to water in my plastic bottle. It was a bit too early for me to be soothing my palate.

Fresh water also came from the winery's fountain for those that did not want any wine. This was a bit of a joyful juxtaposition of water and wine. Echoes of Jesus's miracle of changing water into wine, anyone?

There was a shop near the fountain where I bought a handcrafted necklace with a small scallop shell. It was a small outdoor artisan blacksmith shop where I had a photography playground awaiting me. There was a blacksmith forge, stacked up wagon wheels, chandeliers made from wine bottles, old padlocks—such a cool place.

A little while later, we put our feet up at a cafe in a pueblo called Azqueta to grab some caffeine and cookies. It was pretty windy, but we had a great view of a castle on top of a volcanic-looking mountain. I was praying I wasn't walking up there, but of course, we were.

Except for that initial climb out of Estella, the route was pretty easy through rolling hills of grain, vineyards, and olive orchards. A lot of the way to Los Arcos was many miles with no villages along the way - just putting one foot in front of the other! We continued the walk through the Navarre region.

We met a guy walking the Camino with nothing but a flute and his donkey, Roberto, somewhere. After that, we came upon a woman sitting under a tree playing the accordion with nothing but wheat fields and vineyards for miles in all directions. She was playing for tips, and it looked like she had quite a few. Busking in the middle of nowhere seemed like a tough way to make a living though.

We also found a pop-up bar after miles and miles of nothing where the song "Killing Me Softly" was playing on a loop. I believe it was called Eduardo's café and was a huge American taco-style truck with a few tables in front. He had a never-ending flow of customers. The music was fitting and probably chosen as a cruel joke on all of us. I had a small beer and lemonade here; a Radler, and it was very refreshing! Thank God for Eduardo!

I was dreaming of an Uber as I limped into Los Arcos and climbed up here on the top bunk—as I said, one of the last ones in town. Lina, Maeve, and I decided a rest before dinner would be a good plan. I always volunteered to climb up on the top, as the other ladies were a little older than I was. Some-days this climb up was the last thing I needed.

Directly across from me on another bunk, I saw a woman resting. She had both feet patched up with a combination of Compeed and tape. I knew her from somewhere, and then it clicked. She was the fast-walking, fast-talking woman from the breakfast in St Jean who'd said she was walking 25 miles a day! Well, she wasn't in much better shape than me!

"Hi," I said, "we all started out together at breakfast in St Jean. How's it going? I've got a few blisters too."

"Aren't they just awful things? I'm going to have to take a bus to Burgos and rest up there. Every time I take a step, it feels like someone is slicing the back of my heel!"

"I know that feeling," I laughed.

We all ended up going out for dinner together. The woman named Sally limped along with me. I had pegged her as a bit of a pretentious person, but she ended up being very warm and genuine. Too bad she would be taking the bus, but who knew maybe we would meet again.

The evening was very international with Korean, Japanese, and Swedish walkers, a few Americans, as well as the German girls, Maeve, Lina, and I. We were able to get seated together at a long table, and everyone ordered some kind of meal off the Pilgrim menu.

Dinner was very slow arriving since we were all in such a large group, but it eventually came out. Veal stew, chicken dinners, paella all arrived in front of hungry pilgrims until eventually we had all been served except one young Korean student who waited patiently. He had ordered rabbit stew. Was someone out in the fields hunting for a rabbit?

Finally, with great flurry, we saw a waiter approaching with the final plate of the evening. It was placed almost cere-moniously in front of the Korean pilgrim. We all stared. There, nicely presented on a round plate with carrots and a cilantro garnish, was his rabbit stew. It was a severed head with sunken eyes, and a row of buck teeth swimming in a thick brown sauce. I nearly screamed, but instead I took a large gulp of my Rioja.

"Oh my God!" someone joked, "Bugs Bunny has arrived."

"He wasn't fast enough!" another person added, and we all collapsed into tired and near-hysterical laughter.

"But, he tastes good. Just a little spicy!" the Korean student added, happily crunching on a bony bit.

He ate the rabbit carefully, and seemed to enjoy every single bite. I made a mental note to never, ever order rabbit in a restaurant.

This night I had neither paella nor rabbit. Instead, 14 euros got me chicken and chips, and almost an entire bottle of wine, and a huge slab of cheesecake. The pilgrim meals were good value for money, especially if you considered all that free wine too!

So what had the Camino taught me so far? Enjoy the journey, not the destination, as you never know what is going to be around the next corner. It might even be Bugs Bunny. That's all, folks!

7

LIGHTENING OUR LOADS

DAY 7-LOS ARCOS TO LOGROÑO-28 KM

"Paths are made by walking." - Franz Kafka

The scenery seemed to have changed again. There were a lot of wheat fields, olive trees, eucalyptus, and fields of flowers.

This was the Rioja region of Spain now, and wine was on my mind too! So many hills had terraced vineyards, and they smelled so darn good. Then, walking a little further, we would find yellow buttercups, lavender, and ribbons of wild red poppies. The occasional smells on manure made me notice the scent of the land, not just the sights.

Shortly before Logrono, we came upon a woman sitting under her fig tree and greeting the pilgrims.

"Buen Camino," she said over and over. A small dish sat beside her for donations.

"That's Maria," someone said. "Her family has been doing it for decades."

I looked at her wrinkled face and hands; she was well into her eighties. What must it be like to sit there day after day? It was a tradition and life decision for the mothers in her family, perhaps for generations. Day after day. Some people went into the world, but with Maria, the world came to her. Donations, fortunately, came to her too.

Finally, we got to Logrono. There was a lot of green space, and we strolled along the riverside paths and parks that lined the river bank. It was a beautiful place.

Giant storks flew pterodactyl-like from an island further down the river. They used the city architecture as their nests. They had built large rickety-looking nests atop of bridges, tall buildings, and chimney stacks. These were the first of many storks that we were to see. I later learned that they were partners for life and could live up to 20 years. They must have been quite settled up in the gigantic nests.

Before dinner, we sat in a café in front of the cathedral, watching people walk in and out. I decided to have some "chocolate con churros." This was a typical hot chocolate Spanish treat. The chocolate was served in a cup and was rich and pudding-like, a little too thick to drink. It tasted so good, though, like sweet molten lava. I dipped the "churro"-the finger-shaped light pastry into the chocolate. It was crisp on the outside and tender on the inside, just like all the pilgrims on the Camino.

The albergue in Logrona had a huge room with single beds and lockers in the middle of the room and even some curtains to give yourself a bit of privacy. It was here we first met Raymond. He was also in this large room, and his loud snoring around 5 pm was enough to send Maeve over to shake him awake.

"It's too early to sleep for you," she said, giving his shoulder a shake.

"Hmm," he said, suddenly awake.

"You are a bit of a snorer. I hope you'll be a bit quieter tonight," Maeve advised.

"Um, sorry," he said, waking up a bit and looking at us all staring at him. I have to say he handled this rude intrusion by us all quite well. Waking up to at least five sets of eyes staring at you has to be a little disconcerting.

A little later, we headed off with our recruit to our group, Raymond. We found a restaurant recommended to us because of its famous pilgrim meals.

"Maria!" I yelled as I was walking in. I was surprised that she wasn't further ahead of us since she walked very fast.

"Shannon!" We hugged a bit. Had it only been a week since the train to St Jean? It seemed so long ago. She and a few friends joined us at a large table, and we had a fantastic dinner with paella and delicious cheesecake.

For dessert, we were joined by an Australian couple at the restaurant. They said they were staying by themselves in nice hotels and enjoying a different kind of experience. They seemed a bit lonely, though.

At least in albergues , we met a lot of people every day in the dormitories, or sitting around, or even cooking together. In a hotel, you were isolated, though you didn't have the rustling of bags at 6 am or the snoring to deal with.

It is a personal decision of what is more important. I liked the community of the albergues, but I was not sure that the lack of sleep was worth it. I hoped my earplugs would drown out Raymond's snoring later!

On the way back to the room after dinner, we stopped in at a 500-year-old church and listened to a choir singing a beautiful song. The acoustics were staggering. I'm sure the music brought goose-bumps to us all. Easter would be quite an experience here.

It was nice to meet Raymond this evening. He was an artist from Lafayette and had never been outside of the USA. He loved the Camino and spent time taking pictures of cats, which he hoped to paint later. He very much resembled an artist, with his shoulder-length hair, stubbly face, and stylish clothes.

We were all exhausted and had another huge walk tomorrow. We were getting stronger and slowly used to this new way of life. The guidebook said we had walked 28 km this day. But it felt more like 50! Perhaps John Brierley was a big fat liar, and we had all been sucked into the great mileage lie.

8

THE ALMOND MAN AND IRISH MEN

DAY 8-LOGRONO TO NÁJERA-29KM

"Yesterday is history, tomorrow is a mystery and today is a gift. That is why it is called the present."-Anon.

The walk out of Logroño in the morning was beautiful, past a small lake (some guys were even fishing between the swans) and a park area with eucalyptus trees that filled the air with a minty aroma. There had also been a nice public toilet, that I'd been happy to find. It was a good idea to plan your day around toilet breaks. For example, walk a few hours, have a quick coffee, and use the facilities. You didn't want to have to squat behind a tree too often.

Walking on a path near some farmer's fields in the afternoon, we watched as a small white truck headed toward us. Vehicles were not so common on these side roads, and we stepped aside to let it pass since the road was narrow. As it approached, it slowed down and stopped, and an older man got out. I wondered if Lina had been thinking about her knife!

"Buenos tardes," an older farmer said, and then he added some additional Spanish that I did not understand.

He reached into the back of the truck, "Momento, momento."

Wondering what the heck was going on, we stood there transfixed as he'd reached into a plastic bucket in the back of his truck. What would it be? Fish? Bottles of wine? A rabbit? I was hoping that it was going to be bottles of water; it was so hot.

He held his hands out, and then we did the same as he poured something into them. Not water, however. It was a dozen or so fresh almonds that he poured into our hands. He patted me on the shoulder, looked me straight in the eye, smiled, and said, "Buen Camino." We watched as he drove off.

"Well, that was weird," I said.

"Em, I don't really care for these things," said Maeve. She dumped them into my hands, which were now over-flowing.

"I'll save mine till later," said Lina, putting hers into a side pocket of her pack.

"How do you even eat these?" I said, pouring some into a pocket of my backpack but keeping a few of the fuzzy green shells out. They reminded me a bit of a butterfly cocoon, to be honest.

"You can eat the whole thing."

I popped one into my mouth and bit down gingerly. The shell was a bit bitter, but the inside tasted good.

"Not too bad," I said. "Now we have some snacks if we get hungry. That was nice of that guy."

"Probably his rejects! "I prefer a bit of chocolate myself," chuckled Maeve as she walked on ahead.

I walked with Lina for a bit, and we began to get further and further behind Maeve. She could set quite a pace if she wanted to. We kept walking and, a short time later, we could no longer even see Maeve in the distance.

"Do you think she's OK?" I asked Lina. "She's walking so fast today."

"I think the faster she walks, the happier she is," Lina said.

"Maybe she should walk quickly all the time," I joked.

"That might be best," Lina smiled back. Though we enjoyed walking with Maeve, she could be a little grumpy at times. Of course, Lina and I did have some challenging days too, but for the most part, we all got along very well.

We could see some strangely shaped buildings in the distance, and as we drew nearer, we saw they were strange bee-hive-shaped huts. Resting outside one of them was Maeve.

"You're moving fast today Maeve," I said.

"That would be true. I had to pee, and I didn't want the both of you coming across me with my pants down. I thought these big beehives might be some sort of toilets. They're not; I had to make do with a little bush over there."

"These buildings are *chozo*," said Lina, 'They were a kind of shelter for farmworkers. I read it in my German guidebook."

Lina often availed us with information from her German guidebook. I had exactly the same information in mine, but mostly I chose not to read it. I didn't want to accidentally see the day's elevation maps.

I peeked inside the hut. It was empty except for some food wrappers and a plastic water bottle on the dirt floor. Someone had painted on the old worn stones; a face, the moon, and stars. It was a beautiful and unexpected gallery. Or, if you looked at it another way, a bit of not very good graffiti in a gigantic beehive.

We also spent a good part of the day walking and talking to three sixtyish Irish gentlemen from County Cork, where Maeve was also from.

They were old school friends and had flown to Spain for the past five years to do a section of the Camino. They had completed it once and now had started again from St Jean and were walking as far as Burgos. After that, they would fly back to Ireland and planned to return to walk from Burgos to Astorga next year. Two other friends had walked sections with them in previous years but had now passed away.

"We are doing this walk to Burgos for our old mate, Danny. He did this first little bit from St Jean with us in 2016," one of them told me.

"I thought he'd drop dead there, but he didn't," another of them said, laughing a bit.

"If his wife had agreed to cremate him, we might even have sprinkled him here and there. But, she wanted him 6 foot under!"

They kept up a witty banter as they ambled along with the memories of the old friends they had walked with before. I loved this story and the fact that they could accept their friends' deaths with a good bit of humor. Also, the fact that they kept coming each year to walk a different section was very inspiring.

These guys were great, with no expensive hiking clothes, boots, or backpacks. They were just wearing regular water-proofs, old shoes, and green Ireland baseball hats. They looked like they walked straight out of the pub—but their pace was faster than mine-as was their wit!

We walked with them for part of the day, and then they had walked on ahead after we had stopped somewhere for lunch. But, they were sitting at a cafe on the riverbank in Najere when Maeve, Lina, and I walked wearily into town at the end of the day.

"A little slow, aren't you ladies?" We've been waiting hours for you to have a drink with us!"

"Well, I don't drink, so you'd be eating a long time." countered Maeve. She was as quick-witted as they were.

" Haha. So, where are you ladies staying this evening? The albergue might be a bit too quiet without you."

"Let's keep it that way!" Maeve continued with the banter.

"We are at a guest house tonight," I said. We want to rest up, wash clothes, and chill a bit."

"And not have to listen to any loud snoring!" Maeve struck again.

"Well, truth be told, we only drink enough so we won't hear all that snoring at night, too!"

Such a lot of Irish 'craic' here in Najere it was hard to walk away. But, we did with smiles on our faces and a little more spring in our step.

Najere was a small town squeezed strategically between the river and a dramatic rock face. The action was all around the river with a small merry-go-round and some food stands set up. Helium balloons of Disney Princesses were for sale, and happy children were running around just like children did everywhere. I was tempted to buy a balloon for a laugh and attach it to my pack, in case Maeve and Lina ever lost me.

The town at night seemed much livelier than when we'd entered it in the late afternoon. We ate at a busy, local bar and thought we might run into the Irish trio again, but we didn't.

It was here, in Najere, I learned about tapas. In Canada and the US, I'd never really eaten tapas. In Spain, they are in many bars and significant quantities.

Especially in the cities, you see all sorts of options at the bar when you get your drink. You can just point out a selection of the foods that catch your eye and be handed cute little tapas immediately. In many places, you got free tapas when you order a drink. It might be the bartender's choice, but it's still free food and therefore tastes even more delicious. The little bar we ate at had some of the most beautiful little tapas I had encountered on the Camino.

Lina, Maeve, and I went all out this evening. Mini chicken and peppers kebab, white asparagus (a Spanish favorite) with cheese, tomato and pork, grilled mushroom with shrimp, delicious goat's cheese with nuts and honey, and lots of pork really with anything. They were all delicious. The Rioja wine paired with it all perfectly. It was so nice to have a change from the predictable pilgrim's menu.

We'd all liked Logroño yesterday, but Najere didn't have that atmosphere. Our booking at Hostel Hispano was for a triple room with a TV. The laundry was done and waiting in the room after we got back from dinner. There was a great helpful staff, and it was a nice place to get a good night's sleep. A full stomach helped too.

9

SLUGS, CATERPILLARS, AND A FEW CHICKENS

DAY 9-NAJERE TO SANTO DOMINGO DE LA CALZADA-21 KM

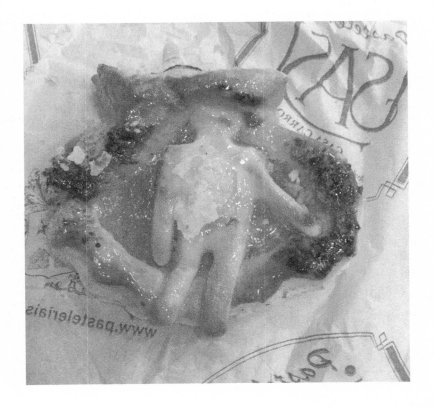

"Walk as if you are kissing the earth with your feet." - Thich Nhat Hanh

We started much later today, around 9 am, and stopped 4 or 5 times for coffee and drinks during the day. We were still walking past vineyards, rolling hills, and vast open spaces. I wanted to put on a sweater and discovered it was not in the pack. It was a favorite, but on the positive side, my pack was still getting lighter.

We walked at a higher elevation, but it was flat for much of the morning. On the horizon, fortified medieval towns appeared miles before you reached them, teasing us. If you blinked, the town seemed further away. Not nice!

A light rain had stopped by the time we got to the deserted town of Ciruena. This was a sterile, empty town with an open country club and several hundred newish condos that were all either empty or had " Se Vende" (for sale) signs on windows or on a post hanging in front. The green and yellow paint on many had already faded, as the hopes of having a community here had obviously never panned out.

We stopped at a golf course clubhouse we found open and ate the only food they had, popsicles, from a large freezer. They were icy cold, just like the town. We started walking as soon as we had used the sparkling clubhouse toilets. They were the best thing about the town.

My blisters were doing much better, and as far as bodily ailments, I was in good shape. However, when I took a break on the trail later, I saw one man limp past with a knee brace. A woman hobbled past in flip flops with her boots hanging from her backpack, and one Korean guy was walking with his heels sticking out over the back of his boots (all one after the other; it seemed like the majority of people were walking stiffly at this point).

I also met a guy walking barefoot. I understood the desire

to feel connected to the earth, but I think the connections with all those sharp stones were too pointed.

We stayed the night in the huge Cofradio albergue in Santo Domingo for 8 euros. There were only ten people in the room, so it was not too crowded. There were lots of comfortable couches to sit in and a huge kitchen and sitting area. We cooked some rice and vegetables with a few Italian cyclists and enjoyed listening to them singing while they cooked. There was a great vibe at this albergue.

An older Italian couple in our dorm was traveling with their border collie, who was resting outside our second-floor window. Dogs were not allowed inside the building. Once in a while, the poor dog started whining and barking, and the Italian guy shouted down at Elmo to stop barking. They said they had walked 42 km today with Elmo - (how is that even possible - I'd walked half that distance, and I was limping around!)

There was a bit of bug action on the trail today. Big, fat, juicy slugs!

These were not cute, tiny, delicate worms. I am talking about fat, ugly, evil things, bloated like stubby black dead fingers wiggling down the path. Some of them had strange, dangerous-looking green unicorn horns on their heads that looked like they could impale other unsuspecting insects. I took several photos since I doubted that anyone would believe their size. In one photo, they were the same length as my sunglasses. Their slow speed reminded me of some slow-moving pilgrims we'd met on the trail.

I didn't see the slugs every day. So did the ever-resourceful French pilgrims delicately scoop them up, put them in a skillet with butter and garlic, and sauté them all, like gigantic escargots without the shells? Or did those Aussie pilgrims, tired of all the pilgrim meals, skewer those slimy slugs and put them on some pilgrim 'barbie' like prawns?

Some days it was the creeping green caterpillars that came

out to play instead of those over-blown black bullets. The caterpillars linked up so that they were thousands of incestuously intertwined moving masses that crisscrossed across the trail and into the grass and trees. It was never just one. They were always in a large group, moving together, never stopping. They were tiny pilgrim caterpillars in a dancing conga line, never stopping and helping one another whether we knew it or not.

Insects were not the only living things on my mind this day. I was also thinking a lot about chickens after I read about a famous 'foul' incident in Santo Domingo.

The legend behind the chickens comes from a story in the Middle Ages. A German family (parents and a teenage son) were attempting the Camino and stopped in Santo Domingo for the night. A flirty barmaid decided she liked the 18-year-old son. However, the boy probably didn't understand her language (or the body language!) or was just not interested and turned her down.

The girl was not happy about this rejection. She put a silver goblet into his luggage, and the next morning the goblet was conveniently discovered missing. She accused the young German boy of stealing, and the boy's bags were examined, and the goblet was found. (Surprise. Surprise!) Soon after, he was brought before the local judge, found guilty, and hanged. That was some fast Camino justice!

The grief-stricken parents continued on their pilgrimage without their son. When they arrived in Santiago de Compostela, they prayed to St James for the soul of their son. On their way back, they stayed the night in Santo Domingo de la Calzada again, and were shocked to find that their son was still hanging from the gallows and, more surprisingly, that he was still alive.

The somewhat traumatised parents rushed to see the judge and explained what they had seen. The judge was miffed that they had the audacity to interrupt his dinner and said, "Your son is about as alive as these dead roast chickens!"

At that moment, the two birds flew off the plate. The more than a little surprised judge was forced to let the boy go.

In memory of this miraculous event, two chickens, have been kept in the ornate gothic henhouse in the cathedral ever since.

Of course, we had to check out this story. So, after our dinner at the albergue, Lina, Maeve, and I took a stroll over to the church. It wasn't far; it was next door.

"Look, it's true," I said, pointing to an illuminated gilded cage high up in the back of the church. Inside there were indeed a rooster and a hen. We could hear them as well. Did they participate in the mass? It appeared the legend did still have some life.

"The chickens are changed, sometimes," another pilgrim also looking at the chickens told us. "Are you guys staying at the Cofradio Del Santo alburgue?" he asked.

"Yes."

"Well, go and look in the back; there is a chicken coop in the courtyard; that's where they get the rooster and hen from. They give the eggs away. You should stop over at that little bakery down in the square; they have some chicken-shaped pastries.

"That sounds a bit strange," Maeve said. "I don't think I need to eat any of those."

I thought the whole story was fascinating, and it made a neat evening outing.

Lina and I walked down to the bakery to check out the desserts. Maeve decided to go straight back. Somehow, I doubt she looked at the chicken coop.

We found the "*milagros del santo*" ("miracles of the saint") chicken pastries and agreed they were good. However, we liked the "*ahorcaditos*" ("little hanged men") even more. These were sweet almond cream desserts shaped like a shell with the shape of a little man resting inside. These seemed a little more bizarre than the chicken pastries. It was a good thing Maeve hadn't come. I'm sure that she would not have enjoyed nibbling on the arm of a little hanged man.

Back at the albergue, we peeked in the courtyard, and sure enough, there was a chicken coop. The 'chosen' ones who were rotated in and out of the church were clucking noisily. That didn't bode well for the morning.

10

THERE'S A SWIMMING POOL ON THE CAMINO?

DAY 10-SANTO DOMINGO TO BELORADO-23 KM

"Methinks that the moment my legs begin to move, my thoughts begin to flow." – Henry David Thoreau

. . .

We were awakened very early this morning to the predictable sounds of the rooster crowing. The cock-a-doodle-do was timed perfectly to the sunrise. There was nothing to do but get up and start walking away from all those chickens.

On the way out of Santa Domingo, we saw more storks near the bridge out of town. Their nests in the church bell towers were massive, and we stood for a few minutes watching the giant birds take off and land.

It was a lovely walk today. There was frost on the ground this morning and snow in the distant mountains with a mist covering the tops of green hills, but it warmed up later.

It was the first day I walked in a T-shirt in the afternoon. Hang gliders and hot air balloons were out in the morning, highlighting the sky with color and a cool slow majesty. What a view that must have been looking down at us all from the sky.

We passed through Granon early in the morning, where I had initially wanted to stay, but it didn't work out. I'd heard that in Granon, there were only a few rooms, and in the attic, you slept on gym mats. The pilgrims cooked the evening meal, cleaned up together, and ate breakfast together. There was a time of reflection at the end of the day and perhaps a sharing of songs and daily memories. It sounded like an incredible experience, and I hoped to find similar albergues somewhere further down the road. The community feeling in the smaller dorms is something that many people on the Camino sought.

We were now in the autonomous region of Castilla y Leon. We checked into a funky place called Cuatro Cantones in Belorado. It had been early afternoon when we'd arrived, and that was lucky. There was a long line of pilgrims; I think because everyone must have read about the swimming pool. Pool party, anyone?

Lina, Maeve, and I got bunks in a small three-bunk room. There was a guy on a top bunk reading a book. It turned out he was from Ireland and was a student. He and Maeve started talking in Irish, and then Maeve stopped talking for a second and started laughing. A real full throaty laugh that I had never heard from her before. She seemed amused about something.

"Do you know what I just heard from Danny, here? Those 3 Irish fellas have gone on ahead by taxi to Burgos. They've been taking a taxi most days, according to Danny! No wonder they always were ahead of us in Najere drinking their beer! The cheek of those buggers!" She laughed, though, and Lina and I did too.

"If I ever see them in Ireland, they'll get a piece of my mind," she added, smiling. I thought they'd probably all get along fine back in Ireland if they ever met. But it wouldn't be in a pub.

Maeve never drank. This was certainly OK by me, but I just wondered why. Was it her choice, or had something happened? I asked Lina about this one day.

" I wondered too," Lina told me. "There's a lot of good wine in Spain she is missing. I'm not sure why she doesn't drink, and I don't want to ask."

"Me, neither."

So, it remained a mystery. Between the two of us, we considered that Maeve's husband had been a heavy drinker or that Maeve herself was a recovering alcoholic (we were pretty sure that this was not true!) We felt that likely that she didn't see the point of drinking. We went with the final option and put up with her disapproving looks now and again.

In the large grassy garden at Cuatro Cuantones, people were stretched out, sleeping, dangling their feet in the pool, or drinking beer from a vending machine in the sunshine. The little pool was enclosed in glass, giving it kind of a greenhouse vibe. You needed a resort wristband for the pool (why?), and you also made reservations for the little restaurant dinner with a set meal. There was a fully equipped kitchen and a laundry room with washers and dryers and many shoeboxes filled with shoes. I felt like we were at a summer camp and had not yet received our Camp Camino t-shirts!

Walking around the town before dinner, it didn't seem like a lot was going on. Of course, there was a little square and a cathedral with mandatory stork nests on top. There were also a lot of murals of flowers and old cars. It was a little odd, and felt a bit like what I imagined a section of Havana might be like.

According to a guidebook, there was a historical point of interest in the alley near some nasty garbage cans where some epic Middle Ages battle took place. I was fast approaching the belief that if I'd seen one epic battle site, I'd seen them all. I came across some murals depicting the epic battle and another point of interest plaque. Belorado must have some epic painters living there.

The little plaza had a small movie theatre, bars, shops, and restaurants. One of them had some crunchy olives that I paired with cheap red wine for a little pre-dinner aperitif. A few nightclubs were advertising openings late at night at 11 pm. But it was very quiet that afternoon. There was more action by the pool. I'd never make it till an 11 pm nightclub, that was for sure!

Dinner in the hotel restaurant was excellent. Here I met Gage from Fargo (not too far from Winnipeg!), who was heading to Thailand to teach English after this walk. I'd taught in Thailand for a while, and he was excited to learn all he could about the country.

"What should I do in Thailand the few days before I start teaching ?" he asked me.

I thought about telling him about the opium-smoking hill-tribe trek, the bars on Pat Pong Road in Bangkok, and the crazy nightlife in Phuket and Koh Phangan. What could I say? Should I prepare him for a bit of a shock from Fargo life? Probably the worst thing he had been exposed to so far in his life were all the crazed Canadians going down to West Acres Mall in Fargo for the holiday sales!

So, I decided to be gentle. "Stay around Khao San in Bangkok, make some new friends, and visit the Palace," I suggested.

He was such a nice young man, and I didn't want him to see too much of Thailand before he had settled in. There would be time for those Lady-boy clubs later!

Back in the dorm, we fell asleep way before nightclub time, but I was awakened by Danny's snoring. I tossed my wet towel over at him. That shut him up for a while!

All snorers should be given a special snorer's room. Maybe they should be locked in too!

"

11

A SAD HISTORY AND AN OASIS

DAY 11-BELORADO TO SAN JUAN DE ORTEGA-24 KM

"Good walking leaves no track behind it."-Laozi

In the morning, I was feeling a little homesick. I'd been gone about two weeks from my husband and daughter. So as we prepared to walk out of Belorado, I told Lina and Maeve I'd catch up to them and made a FaceTime call home.

I knew that my husband and daughter were in Disneyland. Were they even missing me a little?

On FaceTime, they told me excitedly about their day and that they had walked 35,000 steps. This was equal to about as much as I walked some days! The parks were not crowded, and they had been able to go on many rides again and again.

"Are your feet still sore?" my daughter asked.

"Yes, and my blisters aren't getting much better."

"Don't worry; they will. We have sore feet too. We were so tired today we ate a whole XL pizza someplace in about 2 minutes."

I wanted to tell them about the people I'd met, places I'd seen, what I'd learned. But, my experience was hard to put into words. There weren't a lot of XL pepperoni pizzas here.

We talked for a while longer, and I wished that I was in Disneyland too. My favorite attraction was 'Soaring.' This was an elevated ride, where your feet dangled down as you soared over Everest, a waterfall, and other beautiful parts of the world projected in front of you.

That is how I sometimes felt when I walked down the path. It was as if my feet didn't touch the ground.

"Hope you guys enjoy the rest of Disney!"

"We will, and we are following your blog, and it feels like we are walking with you. Love you, Bye."

"Love you too!" FaceTime call ended.

I needed that contact. I wiped a few stray tears from my eyes and followed the backpacks ahead. I could see Lina and Maeve sitting on a bench ahead, waiting for me.

Leaving Belorado, we met a German couple from Bremen who had walked 2800km so far—they had just sold everything they owned and went on the Camino, taking various routes and starting in Le Puy. They hadn't stopped walking for months! It made me wonder where Angelina was.

"Did you ever get lost?" I asked them.

"Many times in France. It was not so well marked there. We used GPS on our phones often. In France, the yellow arrows are everywhere. It is too easy." His wife nodded in agreement.

"The arrows are on walls, rocks, trees, bridges. We even saw one on an old car. I would prefer not such easiness."

"Not me," I said. "I need all the help I can get!"

Some of the Camino arrows were old and quite faded and had a charming age to them, one of many reminders of all the pilgrims who have walked this exact route before us. The yellow arrows had only been painted for the last 40 years.

How had the early pilgrims done it? Had they just followed the stars? It was humbling to think about all the millions of people who must have walked on this same route. We were carrying on a long tradition going back more than a thousand years—so many kinds of people.

We chatted about how horrifying it might be if the Camino became a Disney attraction called the Camino Experience. A log flume ride down the mountains, uphill adventures on Segways, hotels with bunk beds for the real pilgrim experience, and chicken and chips for pilgrim meals. Hopefully never.

Out of town, we started a pretty steep two-mile climb over a rocky trail. On reaching the ridgeline, we were at an oak and pine forest with no views.

The only break was at an Oasis where a woman was selling snacks, fruit, and drinks for a donation. There were some tree trunks and stumps to sit down and rest for a while. It was pretty cool that she gave a fresh piece of watermelon to every passing pilgrim. We left a nice donation for a peach and two bananas.

A bit later, we started the ascent through the village of Villafranca, a steep dirt path entering Los Montes de Oca forest. It seemed to be a logging area as deep truck rutted tracks occasionally led away from the path.

There were astonishing views of the surrounding countryside, but some dark clouds had begun to hover above us. With 12 km left, we were hoping the rain would not come till we got to San Juan de Ortega.

At the top of the mountains was a monument called Monument de Los Caidos. It was a tribute to the 300 victims who were assassinated nearby for their political beliefs during the Spanish Civil War under Franco's regime.

We sat down at some picnic tables to rest for a few minutes. Raymond, Lina, Maeve, and a few other people we were walking with were there. I don't know how it started, but somebody mentioned the Second Word War.

Poor Lina completely broke down, overcome with grief about this period of German history. It was difficult to console her, and I will never forget that place for the heavy feeling of sadness we all felt up there. Lina more than any of us though.

We started a steep descent, crossing a small river and then another steep climb until we reached a pine forest. The walk through the woods was primarily flat but had an eerie feeling about it.

"It's a little spooky in here, isn't it," I said to Maeve. " A bit like that forest near Burguete where I met you."

"You know, Shannon. It has exactly the same feeling. It feels like someone's watching us, that's for certain."

This forest used to be regarded as the most dangerous stretch of the Camino. Along with all the other challenges of the Camino, I just cannot fathom how it must have been for medieval pilgrims to also worry about being attacked and robbed or worse.

I began to feel even more uneasy. I was glad to be walking with Lina and Maeve, and Raymond. We walked mostly single-file, breathing heavily. No birds were chirping, cuckoos cuckooing, and nobody felt much like talking. Something about the road just felt wrong.

It wasn't the first time on the Camino that I'd thought back to medieval travelers walking through the woods. At times, it felt like time overlapping. It was almost as if I was afraid of the past of the woods, not the present. I had definitely watched too many suspenseful movies.

We started envisioning horror film scenarios and found later that many others had shared a similar feeling of heaviness about this stretch of forest, straight out of a Grimm's fairy tale.

The walk lasted almost seven hours. Sometimes I felt like I was drugged. I moved slowly, with my feet crunching on the earth and my poles clacking down. Sometimes that was the only sound.

Walking into San Juan de Ortega with Lina and Maeve, we found out that it was much smaller than we thought. It consisted only of a church, a small monastery, one albergue, one bar, and one casa rural—population 20.

San Juan de Ortega was named for Saint John of the Nettles, who built churches, hospitals for pilgrims, bridges, and hostels throughout this area to improve the Camino for pilgrims. In 1150 he founded an Augustinian monastery in this town.

We found the lovely albergue, El Descanso de San Juan. It was 12 euros with a bathroom in the room and had only been open for five months. It was across from the church. There were even delicious homemade pizzas (though no XL pepperoni), and everyone was so friendly. It was amazing that I had been talking with my family about pizza, and then it was available in a small Spanish town. The Camino provides!

Raymond joined us for that great pizza dinner and told us how cold the monastery was where he was staying. He did mention a delicious garlic soup there, but we were happy where we had ended up.

12

LOST BAGS IN BURGOS
DAY 12-SAN JUAN DE ORTEGA TO BURGOS-26 KM

"No one saves us but ourselves. No one can and no one may. We ourselves must walk the path."-Buddha

. . .

It was a long, slow walk out of San Juan, but it felt a bit like we were flying. We had decided to ship our bags ahead for 5 euros with Jackotrans, to an albergue in Burgos.

This was extremely easy to do. You just put your bag in the lobby, and attached an envelope with 5 euros inside, and wrote the next destination on the envelope. The bag was picked up by a transport van later in the day. They were only going about 20-30 km, so not a bad job for someone. Obviously, though, you needed to know where you would be staying!

With happy light steps, we stopped in the town of Ages to have a coffee at an outdoor café. Soon after, we stopped in Atapuerca for another, as we were feeling a little unenergetic on this day. This was a Unesco Heritage site, as it was the location of the earliest human remains ever found in Europe. We weren't motivated to go to the information center, but it felt special to be treading over the same rocks that many other very ancient feet also had.

We suddenly saw an older woman we had met before. She was walking down the road, looking confused. We had met her once in a faraway village and shared some lentil soup with her, and she had also been in the same room as us in Logrono.

"Hillary!" Lina stood up and yelled and waved at her.

Hillary saw us, and the look of happiness on her face was very apparent as she walked toward us.

"I took the bus from Belorado," she told us, "but I got off at the wrong town. So some construction workers gave me a ride and just dropped me off here. It's a good thing I know a little Spanish!"

She carefully maneuvered her small bag off her shoulders and sat down on an empty chair.

"Where is your nephew?" She had been traveling with him the last time we'd met.

"He was going to walk the whole day today, and I didn't want to walk all 15 miles. Have you seen him?"

"No, not yet."

"So, where were you meeting him today?"

"At a small town called Riopico. But, I think I've missed the way there now."

Lina, Maeve, and I looked at each other.

"We'll walk with you there," we said. "We have all day to get to Burgos."

And so we all set off together over a rocky, hilly path.

"Is this your first Camino, Hillary?" Maeve asked.

Hillary paused for a few minutes at a steep uphill portion to answer.

"I've wanted to come here all of my life. It still does not feel real to me, but my husband passed last year. My church has sponsored me, so here I am, thanks to God."

"How wonderful!" said Lina.

"But, my nephew was worried about me, so he came along. I think that I am fine, though."

"You certainly are!"

"Don't you just love all the beautiful churches we can see here? I have never felt so close to our Lord," Hillary shared.

"It is the same for me," said Maeve.

They walked on ahead of Lina and me a bit, lost in their conversation, the lure of Catholic consciousness bonding them together. They were both kind, wonderful women whose faith was stronger than Lina's and mine. They had already found what they were looking for.

It felt good to be helping Hillary get to her destination. We were happy we had not let her walk alone. It was a very rocky uphill walk and then a slow steep path down. We had to be very cautious of our footing. We took turns carrying her backpack for her. I'm not sure she would have made it without our assistance, but then again, the Camino provides, and something would have worked out for her.

We arrived a few hours later at a small town, and Hillary checked into her albergue, and we sat down to have a drink.

"Thank you so much," she said. "You are my Camino angels today. See you down the road, I'm sure."

I hoped so. She was another person I was delighted to have met.

I think that there's a thing called the *Camino moment*. It's unique to each person walking on the Camino. Some people might have just one moment; others might have a couple, or even many. It's something like an epiphany, a time when you are touched to the core by something you experience on your Camino. I learned so much on my walk this day.

My trusty guide book described the next stretch from there to Burgos as the least pleasant on the whole Camino. And for once, the author had it right. Still, I'd go further and say it was horrible and dangerous, walking along busy roads and through an industrial area.

The walk into Burgos was tedious in that timeless industrial area. The road was long and straight for kilometer after kilometer and busy with large trucks. On the outskirts of town, there was a sign that said another seven kilometers to the old part of Burgos. What? We weren't there yet?

Our detour had put us behind schedule, so we decided to take a bus from Vilafria. This industrial suburb had city buses into the center of Burgos for the last distance, and we would be able to avoid the thunderstorm with lightning that was brewing.

Off the bus finally in Burgos, standing under an awning in a torrential downpour, I thought that Burgos was a beautiful city with a stunning cathedral, shops, and restaurants. The bus had saved us!

We ended up at a place this evening called Hostel Burgos. It was spotless but very spartan and lacked any atmosphere. Worst of all, our bags were not there! Where were they?

A kind staff member phoned around and located them for us. Unfortunately, they had been mistakenly shipped to the municipal albergue, and now we had to go there to pick them up.

We found the other albergue just behind the cathedral. There was a funky restaurant playing Eagles music across the street. I'd like to stay there next time.

I stood staring in awe at both the exterior and interior architecture, sculptures, paintings, stained glass windows, and other art in Burgos Cathedral later. It was very, very impressive. El Cid, the famous Spanish is buried here. I wonder if Charlton Heston researched his starring role in the movie El Cid here?

13

MISSING THE MESETA

DAY 13-BURGOS TO CARRION DE LOS CONDES BY BUS AND TRUDGING ON TO CALZADILLA DE LA CUEZA-18KM

"The world reveals itself to those who travel on foot"-Werner Herzog

I am going to make an admission here that I am not a Camino purist; it is not important to me to put every step onto the ground. A couple of steps onto a bus once in a while is ✓OK! So, with that confessed, we grabbed a multi-city bus out of Burgos and the heavy rain the next day.

One good thing about Hostel Burgos was that it was directly attached to the long-distance bus station. We watched out the window as the outlet malls, car dealerships and gas stations zipped by. We missed a couple of days of the dreaded Meseta. There were no bus tickets left for Maeve, but she would meet us in a few days.

Ah, the dreaded Meseta. Some people loved it, and some people hated it. It reminded me of the Canadian prairies, flat and boring, with lots of pretty yellow crops. It just went on and on like that heart in the Titanic. There were lots of cuckoo birds that seemed to be addressing us directly with 'cuckoo' as we walked. Was this a coincidence or not?

Yes, this was the moment in the Camino we'd all been waiting for—the Meseta in all its Spanish rain-on-the-plain glory. We were just missing the rain! This was the point where you were alone with your thoughts, and suddenly, you had an epic religious revelation. It might even rival that day crossing the Pyrenees suffering hypothermia, thinking you were going to die. But, you survived and lived to tell the stories!

How could mere mortal words ever do this stage justice? It was a venerable paradise for those who are deeply moved by gravel, wheat fields, and blue. Aw, the blueness of it all blue skies, blue feelings and Blues music on Apple music. Did it get any better? I wondered, though, how much monotonous gravel a person was supposed to endure to have an epiphany on that fabulous flatness.

We walked 5 hours from where the bus dropped us at Carrion de Los Condors to a dusty 2 albergues, 3 bars, and one shop town of Calzadilla de la Cueza. It felt like we were in an episode of *West-World* in a dusty, deserted Western town. Were some of these pilgrims actually robots?

There were no coffee shops that I could see, but there was

a small restaurant next door. Thank God I had some chocolate and water. A bunk was cheap, (wonder why?) and we met some great people from Denmark, Hungary, and Ireland once again. Extremely cheap bottles of wine with no labels were available to purchase from a shop that opened especially for us.

Dinner was some Cup Noodles out of a vending machine, and we had a great night hanging out in the courtyard drinking that no-name wine. We thought of a name for it; Meseta Madness. The Danish guy was some sort of marketing guru, and half-drunk told us he'd look into labelling when he got back. So far, I haven't seen that brand for sale at Costco though.

That evening, many people were sitting soaking their feet in bowls of water in the small courtyard. Where else would you have a chance to see big burly men exhausted enough to look like sissies with their tender tootsies exposed to the night?

I do believe there was also a lot of late-night singing too. I didn't love the walking or the scenery this day, but as they say in Star Wars, "the force was strong here," this magical night.

Sitting in the courtyard under thousands of stars that night was unforgettable. We never really learned each other's names, but we didn't need to. We could still connect with each other through stories.

The one I remember the best was some insight from a pilgrim who was walking the Camino barefoot.

"People can't understand why I want to walk barefoot through a path in the forest, through city streets, or in the dust of the Meseta. Mostly it's because I want to be connected to the Earth, and to the other people who have walked here. My feet will take care of me. I feel the Camino everyday!"

His words ' feel the Camino," resonated with all of us, I think, and we all crawled into our bunks, a little quieter than we might have been.

There was a strong snoring force in the dorm this night,

perhaps because of all that wine, and I was happy I had my earplugs.

Yes, the Meseta was the reflective section of this journey. But, as I laid there and reflected, I was glad to think that I was getting closer to Leon. And I was glad to have shoes.

14

A SON IN SAHAGUN

DAY 14-CALZADILLA DE LA CUEZA TO SAHAGÚN-20 KM

"A walk in nature, walks the soul back home." - Mary Davis

We were all up early because of the snorers! This morning, in the shared bathroom, while brushing my teeth, a woman, possibly hung-over, suddenly got dizzy, hit her head on the sink, and fell to the floor unconscious. With toothpaste foaming at our mouths, a few of us hauled her up to a sitting position and concurred that the gash in her head didn't look that deep. Someone found her husband, and she regained consciousness with just a little blood dripping from her head. She seemed to be ok.

"What happened!" her husband shouted, as he came running into the women's toilets.

"Don't know," she said.

"Can you get up?"

"Yes, I think so."

We hauled her to her feet, and walked her carefully down to her bunk.

"Thank you everyone. I'm fine. Just tired, and I need something to eat."

Someone found her an energy bar and a Sports drink and we left her and her husband to talk.

I saw her with a few Compeed blister patches stuck to her head later a bit later. She was packing up her bag and getting ready to start off with her husband. She wasn't giving up, but I strongly suspected it wouldn't be a late gin and tonic night for her. Water, a lot of it, would be her best choice.

It seemed like almost everyone was suffering from something at this stage; sore feet, blisters, taped-up knees and ankles. But, like good soldiers, we trudged on, not complaining, ready to support one another, pushing our bodies to their limits in some cases. Though not as hard as the barefoot walker, who was long gone.

I walked with a Danish girl and swapped a few travel

stories this morning. She had volunteered for quite a while in India, and we both spoke of our love for that country. This was the third section of the Camino that she had done. She was wearing an identical necklace to the one I bought at the small blacksmith's shop near Irache fountain on the 6th day of the walk. She said she hadn't taken it off in 3 years and had bought hers at precisely the same place. Though I take mine off from time to time, it too remains my favorite purchase on the Camino.

This was Knights of Templar territory. It was these✓ knights who protected the pilgrims from robberies and murders. For centuries their order has been steeped in legend, myths, and mystery. Some scholars think they had a noble mission to protect pilgrims on the various pilgrimage routes across Europe. That was true, but it was not their only role. One of their prominent roles had been to serve as troops in the Crusades too. History suggests they were not always good guys here. A lot of mystery shrouds this order; but I like to think of them as the protectors of the pilgrims.

I wouldn't say I liked the look of Sahagun when we walked in. The town square was small, and it was a desolate, medium-sized city in the middle of nowhere. We had to wait for the municipal albergue to open, but it was nice enough inside. It was a vast dorm in an old church, and friendly people were staying near us. Maeve caught up to us here, as she had taken a later bus from Burgos. The gang was back together.

In the bunk next to mine, I met an Italian mother in her late 20s that I will never forget. She was finishing blow-drying her hair and putting on a bit of mascara when I met her. It had been a long time since I'd done that.

"Do you have any ideas about a place for dinner?" I asked.

"Sure, I'm a-gonna go to the Michelin place, Luis's, I heard about." She had a great Italian accent; she was from Rome.

I thought she was joking, but sure enough, a little while later, a group of 10 or so of us trekked to a restaurant just off the main square. There was an actual Michelin sign, no stars but still, Michelin!

I'd love to say it was a fabulous dinner, but it wasn't. Maybe we caught them on a bad night. I had some sort of chicken (it could have been an old shoe); it was quite chewy and served with soggy fries. We did have several good bottles of wine with the meal that were not included. No pilgrim's meals at this Michelin place, so a little pricey for this pilgrim crowd. But it was a nice place for us all to be together at a large round table.

The Italian mother's name was Simona. She texted continuously through the meal and apologized non-stop.

"I'm texting my son; he is 13. I have to make sure he does his homework and is helping his sister. She is 8; she misses me very much." She had tears in her eyes, and all the wine that we were drinking was not helping her raw emotions this evening.

"The Camino has been calling me, and I needed to take the time to do this. I am walking as fast as I can. I hope that I can finish in another nine days. I miss my husband and kids so much!"

I did some mental calculations; it would take me more than two weeks to get to Santiago. So I guessed I wouldn't see Simona any time soon.

Also at the table, that evening was Tomasso. He was from Italy, too. He and Simona spoke English with us but once in a while would talk among themselves in Italian. Tomasso was soft-spoken, slow-moving, and had very little money. He shared the wine and had only nibbled on the complimentary bread.

I'd seen him when he'd arrived at the hostel. He was impossible to miss. The pain of each step was written unforgivingly across his sweat and dust-marked face as he walked to his bed. He sat on it, slowly unwinding the surgical tape that he had bound his feet with. He told me that he had come up with the idea of binding his feet with surgical tape because an old pilgrim had told him it could prevent blisters. I wasn't sure about that, and his feet were very swollen from the tightness of the tape.

During a lull in the conversation, he began to speak about himself. I thought about his painfully swollen feet.

"I can feel Simona's pain. She is a mother, and I am a son. We do this walk for ourselves and our families. It is a matter of pride. She wants to walk quickly, but I want to walk slowly. We all have our own pace. And, without separation, sadness, and pain, the Camino is not as meaningful."

We were all silent; it was such a poignant moment. How wonderful those words must sound in Italian.

We all chipped in and bought him a dinner that evening. It was the least we could do. Simona and Tomasso had made us understand the value of the Camino a little more that night.

After dinner, our little group went to listen to some cloistered nuns sing. This was not high on my list, but Maeve and Lina wanted to attend.

We went to a Benedictine monastic complex that was once the biggest in Spain. All that remains now is a clock tower, an ancient church, some well-preserved ruins, and a small convent of a dozen or so Benedictine nuns who watch over the remains.

We joined a small, seated congregation in one of the rooms. The nuns were out of sight (as all cloistered nuns should be), but their voices were piercing and exquisite during the evening vespers at 7 pm.

"Maeve, that was amazing. How did you hear about this?" I asked her as we were walking back to the albergue.

"My son attended when he did the Camino a few years ago. He told me not to miss it, and I'm glad I listened to him this once," she chuckled.

Back at the hostel, we all went to sleep pretty fast. But I could see the light of Simona's phone under her sheet. What a firm pull the Camino had on her to leave her husband and kids to walk. And she had enough room in her backpack for a hair-dryer to still look good while practically flying down The Way. Tomasso would be moving more slowly.

15

WHEN BLISTERS SPEAK

DAY 15-SAHAGUN TO RELIEGOS 3OKM AND A BUS TO LEON

"Make your feet your friend." – James M. Barrie

In the morning, Simona and even Tomasso were long gone. Some people planned to walk some extra miles across town to Iglesia Señora La Peregrina to get a Carta Peregrinas. This was a certificate written in Latin that stated that they had reached the halfway part of the Camino. We decided to keep going. We'd get our Compostela at the end. It was good enough to know that we had made it to the halfway mark.

The Meseta was a bitch! Lots of bits of old Roman roads, so very straight. I sometimes looked for the glint of ancient Roman coins between the stones but had found none so far.

Dirt fields, wheat fields, no cafes, and a few picnic tables in the middle of nowhere were the scenes of the day. But there was a quiet beauty in the crumbled adobe buildings that were like old skeletons picked dry and now bleaching in the sun. There were no buildings or homes in the fields. Instead, people seemed to live in the dying towns and drive out to the fields to care for their land. It was their way.

Even though I didn't walk all the Meseta, I could see the value of the reflective time.

I reflected now on my feet. I hadn't taken care of them enough. I should have listened back in Pamplona when I was told to pierce them and put a thread into them. I should have taken my socks off more often and taken care of hot spots immediately. Again, I should have listened to my feet.

So, I now found myself having to hobble into the Meseta paradise of Reliegos. Maeve and Lina were at least 30 minutes ahead of me and sitting on the street at those ubiquitous red plastic cafe tables when I got there. Although they were at least ten years older than I was, they walked a lot faster and complained a lot less. They also did not have any blisters.

I gasped a quick "Hi, thanks for waiting," dropped my bag beside their table, and practically crawled past them into the restaurant. The female bartender was pouring whiskey shots for someone. I very nearly ordered a shot (I was tired but still focused)—but it was still early.

"Cerveza por favor," I croaked.

I sat down at a stool at the bar to wait for it, took off my shoes, and peeled off my socks. Unfortunately, they were a little stained with blood and stuck to my ankle. People did this naked feet expose all the time on the Camino. In fact, I think I had first been introduced to this stripping method by my Dutch hippy way back near St Jean.

The smiling middle-aged woman put my beer in front of me and peered at my raw naked feet, which were dangling down like fine pieces of ham in a Spanish butcher shop.

She held a hand to her mouth and said something like "Madre de Dios!" which I could understand quite well.

I looked at her and sort of shrugged my shoulders and would have said, "What can you do?" but I didn't know the Spanish. So I just said. "Otra cerveza por favor," as I downed the first one. It was just a tiny glass.

She turned back to pour my beer, and I tried to put a couple of Compeeds on the back of my heels. When I looked up again, she was back with a larger beer and a shiny knife.

She mimicked a cutting motion on my feet. I knew that some people had blisters completely cut off, but she didn't seem like the right person to do it. So, I just said, "No gracious," and we both had a nice laugh together.

I carried the beer outside and hobbled barefoot to meet the other two with my shoes and socks under my arms. I dug my sandals out of the backpack and felt a bit better. But, it was starting to drizzle, and I wouldn't be able to wear them in the rain.

"Hey, it's all right if you guys walk ahead a bit. I have to take care of my feet. I'm going to go to a Farmacia and see what they have. I can't walk in my shoes much longer."

"We will wait for you, Shannon." People on the Camino were very loyal.

I got a pharmacist's recommendation on disinfectant, moisture-licking insoles, blister bandages, and stocked up on Compeed, antiseptic and surgical tape. After that, I felt prepared for battle.

Back at the bar, I borrowed a pair of dull scissors from the bar lady to cut a new pair of insoles down to size. Eventually I had hacked at them enough and they fit into my shoes. I tried a few steps. A little better.

A random older Spanish man had come in and was now sitting at the bar eating a Spanish tortilla. A Spanish tortilla looked a bit like a quiche and was made with potatoes and egg.

The old guy stopped eating his tortilla, beckoned to me, and said, "Mira, Mira." (That meant 'look,' didn't it?)

Then with one quick motion he reached into his coat pocket and pulled something out slowly and carefully, like a magician pulling a rabbit from a hat. Perhaps he had been hunting in Los Arcos recently?

It was an unused women's maxi pad. How bizarre was this day?

I just stared at him, a bit dumbfounded. I really had no words in English or Spanish.

He took a guilty, secretive look around the bar to make sure no one else had seen him pulling maxi pads from his coat. Because really, how does one explain that? He tucked it away again as several more customers came in through the door.

When no one was watching, he motioned to me to take my shoe off. Then, he showed me how to put the maxi-pad under the insole and had me practice walking across the bar. I had to admit; it felt springy and comfortable. So now I had new gel insoles, cushiony maxi pad support, and more blister bandages on my heels.

The blisters on the bottom of my feet I could deal with now. However, it was the back of my heel blister rubbing on my shoe that was painful. There were no maxi pad supports for that location, sadly.

I bought the guy a beer and then paid my tab to the knife-wielding woman. I liked this little place. But why did a man in a little rough Spanish bar have a maxi-pad in his pocket?

I could only imagine that he came in there specifically to help people with their aching feet, hoping to get a free glass of beer. It was a unique line of business.

I had to put my sandals on to walk in, though (no maxi-pads there). I didn't think I could handle the sharp pain from the heel blisters. When I got outside, the skies opened, and the rain came pouring down. I talked Maeve and Lina into taking a cab into Leon since it was raining very hard now. The driver had us there in 20 minutes, dry and happy. I didn't feel guilty at all for taking a taxi; my feet deserved a break.

Leon was insanely busy. It was the Easter celebration week (Semana Santa), and we had a lot of trouble getting a bed. We hadn't planned to be here this early in the day, but it was very, very lucky we took that cab and got into Leon before the beds were all gone. Things happen.

We must have been looking lost, because a kind priest had come up to us and offered to help us. He'd led us to the municipal albergue run by Benedictine nuns, in a twisted mess of back alleys. There was a dorm for men and a dorm for women here. There also seemed to be one for families, which was where we ended up. It was full of Spanish families in town to see the Easter celebrations, and it looked like it would be quite the experience.

The streets of Leon were full of people drinking and celebrating the upcoming Easter. We were so lucky to have a bed.

16

SEMANA DE SANTA IN LEON

DAY 16-LEON

"If you are seeking creative ideas, go out walking. Angels whisper to a man when he goes for a walk." - Raymond Inmon

. . .

We were awakened at 5:00 by people who had turned on all the lights and were repacking their plastic bags, rustling those plastic bags, and talking loudly. That seemed hugely inconsiderate, but I tried thinking good Camino thoughts.

When I could no longer handle it, I said, "Shhhh!" Very loudly.

A woman paused to look up at me, actually smiled, and went back to packing up. There was nothing to do except to get up.

Breakfast was by donation in a small breakfast room. There were baskets of bread and jars of jam and instant coffee. We squished in at the table and ate all we could. Everyone seemed to be leaving 5 euros, so we did the same.

We talked to a girl from Barcelona who was here for the Easter processions. She said Seville and Leon were particularly good places to experience the processions and that not all areas of Spain have elaborate celebrations. We realized how truly fortunate we were to get a bed last night.

"You are refreshed and slept well?" a four-foot nun clad in layers of starched clothing said to me as I shouldered my bag off the bunk.

"Oh yes, it was wonderful." I probably shouldn't have lied to a nun, but there were no immediate signs of lightning outside that might strike me.

Outside the front door of the albergue, an Easter procession was walking past the entrance. Talk about a good location and good timing.

We stood to the side of the street with hundreds of others and watched. It was very impressive, memorable, and solemn. The floats jerked slowly past us, carried on the shoulders of strong, steadfast men. Each elaborately carved wooden float represented a different station of the cross and contained realistic Jesus and Mary statues, decorated with candles and flowers. The Catholic past lived on!

They were accompanied by spirited music (played on

saxophones, trumpets, and drums) by hundreds of "Nazarenos" (penitents) wearing pointy hoods and cloaks in various color combinations.

Another procession included widows wearing black clothing. Some were weeping. It seemed like an intrusion for us to be participating in this painful moment. Yet, we couldn't look away, nor could other Spanish spectators. It was an unforgettable 90 minutes.

Many participants were wearing unique pointy hats — that looked a bit reminiscent of American KKK hoods, so I looked up what the significance was. It seemed they were called "capirotes" and were used during the times of the Spanish Inquisition as a punishment. People condemned had to wear a paper-made cone on their heads with different signs on it, corresponding to the type of crime they had committed.

Centuries later, people started to use them during Easter processions to symbolize their status as penitents. Today, the capirote still shows an attempt to get closer to God. It also covered people's faces in order to mask their identity.

They looked a little medieval. Small kids and adults alike were hooded and solemn. It seemed more like a procession to the gallows than to an Easter celebration.

The entire city seemed to participate. Whole families, from babies to grandparents, and many groups of young and old, came out into the street, especially in the late afternoon and evenings. I felt very fortunate I got to experience this day. I had no plans to be in Leon now, but several people mentioned this spectacle. I was so glad it had all came together. I could thank my blisters!

The next day, our luck held, and we got three beds at another place, the San Francisco Asissis albergue. There was even an elevator here; a room for four people was 12 euros each. They had a small cafeteria, and breakfast was cheap here. It was run by some Franciscan brothers who gave us a quick tour. Nuns, monks, Easter ceremonies, I was practically born-again!

In the afternoon, I finally bought some more new sneakers at a cheap shoe shop. Later, I walked past a little Chinese restaurant, then turned around and walked inside. Then I heard myself ordering the number 2 chicken mixed vegetables. I practically inhaled it. Honestly, I felt like I should be eating 'real' Spanish food every day, but I just felt a sudden craving for the oyster sauce and a large quantity of unhealthy MSG.

The pilgrim meals with their predictable choice of a salad, a selection of chicken, pork chop, and custard for dessert were getting monotonous. Although, the free wine was still the big draw for me!

Just before dinner, a Franciscan brother gave us a tour of the church and monastery. There used to be over 100 brothers, and now there were only around 7. They continued to help families in the community and ran the albergue here. He told us to look to our inner selves on the last stage of the journey and, like St Francis of Assisi, to connect more to nature on the last stage of the Camino. OK, maybe my Camino for my mind was coming into focus after all!

It was a lovely, relaxing day. My feet felt much better, and I felt like I could walk for the next two weeks! Perhaps we would meet the king and queen of Denmark, who had been on the news since they had been spotted on the Camino. If they were smart, they would have thrown some of those hoods over their heads and gone incognito in the streets of Leon!

17

LAZY DAY IN LEON
LEON

"Look deep into nature and you will understand everything better." - *Albert Einstein*

The next day, I decided to spend the morning in my top bunk in the small eight-bunk dorm room and give my blisters time to heal! We were on the third floor, and I could look down to the street and see crowds of people and hear the sad processional music once again. The celebrations were sporadic and at different times and on many streets. The city was still absolutely heaving with people.

The night before, simple mattresses had been placed on the floor in our room to fit in four more people. But, of course, you had to be careful not to step on someone's head if you needed to go to the bathroom!

I scrolled through my phone at a few Camino Facebook groups I belonged to. The groups were for people planning the Camino and for those who were currently walking to post information. Both were incredibly helpful.

For the past few weeks, the Facebook groups had detailed thefts of phones and some money from hostels. There was speculation it was a gang posing as pilgrims. The thefts were a few days behind me- but we were still careful with valuables. My money belt was always with me. But thieves were slashing sleeping bags because a money belt was often hidden by pilgrims at the bottom of a bag. I couldn't understand how people did not wake up! Anyhow, I'm pretty confident everyone in our room was a pilgrim. I didn't think thieves would enjoy sleeping on the floor that much.

The Facebook groups were beneficial, too, if you were nervous about the Camino. People asked all sorts of questions, like if they should 'go commando' and wear no underwear, or they wondered how best to tie shoelaces or what color socks to bring. Questions were answered kindly and thoughtfully. Everyone had a different comfort level, and it took longer for some people to adjust to this daily life.

I would have been more nervous on this journey if I had never backpacked. I thought it was essential to stay in the albergues to rough it a bit and to be on the same level with everyone. I guess it can be a little disconcerting to sleep in a mixed dorm room with people from all over the place. Let me say those French men are not at all shy!

By late morning, I couldn't stand it in the room any longer and decided to break free. I put on my sandals and tried not to aggravate the blisters. I went to a few museums and the cathedral here. It was probably the most impressive cathedral I have ever been inside. There was beautiful stained glass with still very vibrant colors and incredible wood carvings and stonework. On the whole, Leon's Cathedral was not as grandiose or artistically stunning as the cathedral in Burgos. However, it had an impressive Gothic style, which made it memorable to me.

Of all the architectural wonders in Leon, the one that has stayed with me the most is the Basilica de San Isidoro. It is a small and sturdy little museum attached to the church. I met Maeve there, and we were fortunate to go on an English tour. The real showstoppers here were the cloisters and Royal burial vault known as Pantheon Real, where assorted royal remains are buried. But I preferred to look up at the fabulous artwork on the ceiling. The frescoes on the ceiling and walls were 800 years old, unrestored but still vivid. The life of Christ was detailed in muted colors. Its nickname is Spain's, Sistene Chapel.

The chalice of Dona Urraca was also here. It became famous when it was considered to be the Holy Grail at one time. Could this have been the chalice used by Jesus at the Last Supper? It looked more like a prop in a high school theatre production, to be honest.

The most impressive things here for me were the thousands of ancient books in a small one-room library. The Leon Bible of 960 A.D, with colorful scenes of the New Testament, was opened here in a display case. Centuries-old, colorful gilded pages of medieval life were preserved forever. Everything was under glass or sealed off, but it still smelt old and musty and full of mystery and history in that little room.

This Basilica also housed the bones of San Isidoro, a 6th-century archbishop. It had become a pilgrim stop on the way to Santiago, and many pilgrims came to view the relics. A Door of Forgiveness was also found here where pilgrims who were too sick to get to Santiago were "forgiven."

The whole historic area is worth just sitting in and soaking it up. The day was sunny, so I did just that. Nice to be a tourist and not a pilgrim for a day!

I walked a little further and started talking to another pilgrim at a park who said since we slept in a different city and different beds on the Camino each night, so there was no real sense of home, so home became something that you carried inside you. So maybe that's why I hadn't felt particularly homesick so far.

But, with really nothing to do today, I felt like some comforting caloric taste of home. So, I did what anyone would do in such a situation; I went to McDonald's!

I ordered a cafe con leche and a burger and fries. It wasn't cheap or as large as a pilgrim's meal, but it was a nice change. It tasted just as I knew it would. The building was new, beautifully decorated, right on the river bank, and seemed very upmarket. There were lots of well-dressed Spaniards inside. There were also several pilgrims there. I could pick them out from their wrinkled clothes and dirty shoes. We avoided eye contact. Nobody wanted to admit to being there. It was not the homeless crowd that McDonald's can attract at home.

Double confession time. I also went to Carrefour Express. This is a popular grocery store chain, a French version of

Walmart. While there, I saw pilgrims swarming the aisles and throwing things gleefully into baskets. People were grabbing clothes, shoes, batteries, anything they thought they needed and were willing to carry. They seemed intent on grabbing things they had not eaten for some time—lots of fresh fruit. I grabbed kiwis, strawberries, blueberries. Who cared what it cost! It was every pilgrim for themselves as we loaded up on anything that did not in any way resemble a pilgrim's meal. I also grabbed some excellent cheese, yogurt, and multi-grain bread. The cheese counter and the meat counters were like mini-stores within this grand hypermarket.

Later, I was sitting on my top bunk, examining my spoils, strawberries in hand (and excess juice on my face), when Lina and Maeve returned to the room.

"Guess who we just met?"

"No idea," I replied. "The Prince of Denmark? Are we be meeting him for drinks later?"

"No, we just ran into Angelina from Pamplona!" said Lina. "And, she suggested drinks later at a tapas bar."

Angelina! I thought. Fantastic.

"Sounds great!" I said.

I glanced over at Maeve, who was tight-lipped.

"I won't be going with you this evening. I'll look forward to hearing more when you get back."

That was the end of the Angelina subject with Maeve, that was for sure.

After a hot shower and with my cleanest pants and shirt on, Lina and I headed out to our tapas bar rendezvous. I spotted Angelina right away, smoking a cigarette, with a funky scarf draped around her neck and lots of silver in her ears and on her hands. Several Spanish men were stealing glances at her.

She burst into a radiant smile as she spotted us.

"Oh my, Shannon! "I am so happy to see you again." She squeezed me so hard; I could hardly breathe.

"Thank you for coming back, Lina!" And she squeezed her, too.

"Where is Maeve?"

"Sorry, she's too tired. She likes to go to sleep early."

"And, she might stop us from a little fun too?" she added with a little wink.

We settled down at a dark table, and ordered a bottle of red and grabbed some tapas.

"So, where have you come from, Angelina? And, where are you going?"

"Well, I am in Leon for Semana Santa. It is amazing, yes? I am now going to Hospital de Orbigo where I will meet a new friend. Can you guess who it is?"

"I have no idea. We've met very different people, I think."

"I will give you a hint. He is handsome, kind, and from Italy."

That could only be one person that I knew, "Tomasso?" I tried.

"Yes, he is my Camino angel. He told me that he had met all of you a few days ago."

"Ha," I said, "it's nice to be remembered." So what was up with her and Tomasso, I wondered? Just friends?

"Will you both volunteer?"

"Yes, my friend is there in Hospital de Orbigo at Albergue Verde, and we will volunteer with him. You must come and stay."

"I will, of course," I said.

"I'll see what Maeve wants to do," said Lina.

OK, I had to ask. "Angelina, things are a little awkward with you and Maeve. How come?"

Lina looked down at her feet, not wanting to get drawn into a conversation about Maeve. I just wanted everyone to be friends; I cared about them all.

Angelina took a long drag on her cigarette and then answered. "I am not certain, but I think I remind her of herself. And, maybe I am too loud and too crazy for her. I am her bad side. I have made mistakes, and I think she has too. I drink too much sometimes, which she does not like. Sometimes, I am a little sad. I think Maeve is sad inside too. She doesn't like what she sees when she looks at me."

"Aw," I said. "Maybe you two could talk about something and find some common ground. It would be great if you both got along."

"No, I don't think Maeve will do that. She does not like to look back. And, I don't think we will see each other after the Camino. So, it is no problem."

And that was the end of that discussion.

We talked more about Tomasso, and I could see that Angelina wanted to help him along the Camino. Unfortunately, neither had much money, and volunteering at the albergue would only give them food and a place to stay for a while. Maybe it was enough for the both of them for a time.

Lina, Angelina, and I closed out the night with some wine and lots of laughter. I promised to see her in a few days. Lina could not make such a promise.

Back in the room, it was challenging to step among the sleeping figures on the floor. I climbed gingerly up the ladder onto my top bunk, taking care not to put too much pressure on the blisters on the bottom of my feet. All of us were spread out, sleeping, like the frescoes of the ordinary people in the Basilica de San Isidoro.

18

GOOD-BYES

DAY 18-LEON TO VILLAR DE MAZARIFE-22 KM

"An early-morning walk is a blessing for the whole day." – Henry David Thoreau

We left Leon the following day at about 8 am; the yellow arrows directed us past the Cathedral and the main historical district and through the outskirts, past the cheaper housing, the car dealerships, dirty factories, and finally into the countryside. There were some exciting moments of dodging fast-moving trucks and cars, trying to figure out which side of hell the arrows wanted you to be on. One minute we were on one side of the busy highway, and the next, that flipping arrow had us playing chicken with a car crossing over to the dark side.

Today we had a choice of following the shorter Camino (but just a path beside the highway) or an alternative route (across the country). We decided to try the alternative way, and it was a great choice.

Remember your Robert Frost. "Two paths diverged in the woods, and I took the one less traveled, and that has made all the difference."

Soon we were walking over scrubby oak, brush, and an occasional harvested field. Nobody seemed to live around here. It was quiet-just the sound of our feet crunching on gravel and the poles hitting the ground.

Some enterprising guy had set up an orange juice bar (think power cord and cheap juicer) with bananas, Nescafe, and chocolate bars for sale on the way out. In addition, there was a tiny toilet in his office available for use, which was much appreciated.

My new bright-blue shoes were not doing me any great favors. Each step still felt like someone was taking a knife to my heel.

We came down a big hill where another smart business guy had set up a coffee shop at the bottom of the hill. This was our 2nd pit stop; 4 hours were done. Lina and I sat slurping steaming cups of coffee. Maeve insisted on tea with extra hot water and lemon on the side. We sat at tables on a small terrace that was also occupied by ageless Spanish men playing chess. They barely glanced at us, or the other walkers who walked past us and waved.

We continued moving to another town and found a lovely little cafe that had brown bread. We hadn't seen bread this color in a long time. Yes, we had enjoyed many *"bocadillo"*; a baguette sliced lengthwise down the middle and stuffed with a choice of either ham or other meats or cheese. But, we were a little sick of baguettes. So, brown bread was very exciting!

And, there was also a special on Sangria? My goodness, we had not seen that for ages either. I tried to order a small glass, but they only had "grande" Oh well, sometimes you have to adapt.

It was a lovely lunch of brown bread and Sangria.

I decided to bring up the Angelina issue.

"So, Angelina and Tomasso are volunteering at Verde hostel in Hospital de Orbigo. I think I'm going to stay there for a few days."

Maeve took a slow sip of her orange juice. "Jaysus, Shannon, I can't stand that woman. I don't know for certain why, but she rubs me the wrong way, with all her talk of lost children, and here she is walking back and forth across Spain doing nothing. And, Lina tells me now she has trapped our Tomasso in her web. It just all makes me a little sick."

Lina was looking at her hands after Maeve's little unexpected outburst. I would have liked to have focused on my hands too, but I had stepped into it now and would have to focus on my mouth.

"Um," I tried, "I can understand that. But I think she's been through a lot in her life, and I don't think she is a bad person. I think she's just had some bad luck."

"Er, that's for sure. Bad luck that she has made a bit of herself. I think that she has never grown up and has left her family high and dry. She's irresponsible, that one. Well, let's not worry about her now. We'd best all be off."

End of conversation.

We gathered our bags and poles and headed away from the main square.

"No, No!" many Spanish men were shouting at us and waving their hands. Did they want us to drink some more Sangria?

Nope. They were pointing too. We had headed in the wrong direction. And I'd only had one grande glass of Sangria. Still, it was a little embarrassing.

We walked for a while in silence, and I gave what Maeve had said some thought. I knew what she said about Angelina was true, but I still thought she was a very genuine but damaged person. She was also a lot of fun to be with. Despite her life, she was still very positive.

It was Maeve who was getting on my nerves a bit.

According to the guidebook, we had passed through three peaceful little villages. I shall remember one for the power juicer, one for the chess players, and one for the brown, brown bread.

We got to Villar De Mazarife about 3:30. I had listened to some music for a while, but otherwise, we walked in silence. I had downloaded a lot of music with walking themes. Somedays, I could liven myself up with "Walking on Sunshine" or "Walk Like an Egyptian." Today was a "Let it Be" and the "Sounds of Silence" sort of day.

We had planned to stay at the Jesus albergue and walked over to look at it. It was a huge place, but I think we got there at a bad time. The owners were eating and didn't want to deal with us. We were given a brief tour of the rooms, and then they went back to eating and watching a soccer game on TV.

We went back to walking, but just across the street, because the Jesus place didn't give us the right vibes. The Antonio de Padua albergue, on the other hand, was great! We were given three beds in a small dorm and had the whole room to ourselves. Maeve and Lina decided to have a nap, and I went down to the kitchen to see if I knew anyone staying here.

Three guys and one woman were sitting around a long table reminiscing about their day. They asked me to join them, and I found out the men were from New York and the woman was a Canadian from Nova Scotia.

I had met very few Canadians on my walk so far. I don't know why, just timing, I suppose.

"We were just talking about the truck stop breakfasts we have," Nancy the Canadian said. "Mostly, it's just Nescafe, cigarettes, and a chocolate bar."

"That doesn't sound great," I laughed.

"Yes, but it is quick!" she giggled. She was in her fifties, very thin and fit, and looked like she could handle anything that was thrown her way. It looked like one of those New York guys had been thrown her way. They seemed to be an item.

"We like to start walking at about 5 am," she continued, "sometimes there's nothing open. If we are near a city, we always head for a gas station and get caffeinated and sugared up. It's the best time to walk. No one is around yet, and you can power through the miles. We just put our head-lamps on and keep an eye out at our footing if we are in the hills."

"Sounds a bit dangerous; must be peaceful, though," I said. "I don't think I could get up that early."

Honestly, I was thinking how very glad I was they weren't in our dorm if they were up before 5 am rustling in their bags!

"Sure, you should try it. We even got this older lady and her nephew to join us one morning back in Najera."

"That must have been Hillary and her nephew, right? We met them in Logrono and then in Atapuerca. She's great. Isn't she in her eighties? How is she doing?"

"I know, right? We had such a special walk with her and her nephew. We all got breakfast together that morning as the sun came up, and she said a special prayer with us. You heard she had to go home, right?"

"No, I didn't! Oh no! What happened? We haven't seen Hillary since near Burgos!" I was devastated to hear this bad news about Hillary.

"Well, I think she was getting tired and confused because she wasn't getting enough sleep in the dorms. She was still game enough to crawl up on a top bunk. But her nephew decided she'd had enough and bussed them both to Santiago to fly home. It might have been a bit too much for her, with her backpack and all the long days."

"She was so inspirational, carrying her own stuff, getting everyone to pray together, and being so positive. I hope she is ok. We all loved her positivity," I said.

"Yes, she was someone special, that's for sure!"

It was sad to hear about Hillary since she had told us that it was her life's dream to walk the Camino. She had walked several weeks of it, and those weeks had not been easy. But it was wonderful that she had gotten as far as she did. I've never forgotten that day walking with her on a stony path up and down the steep hills.

I went back to the dorm and told Lina and Maeve about Hillary, too. Like me, they were disappointed but had been impressed by her.

"She went as far as she could. You can't do more than that," said Maeve quietly. "We are lucky to have met her."

Pepe, the owner of the albergue, was also another extraordinary person that I was lucky to have met. He was seriously ill when he was young; he promised back then if he got well, he would open a hostel and give the pilgrims a home. And that is what he did. Now, he gave energy-force-circulation healing treatments too for a small fee. I had one of these massage treatments, and I can honestly say I felt energized.

A little later, we went back down to dinner. About 20 people were there that night, and we were served soup, salad, paella, strawberry crepes, and all the wine we wanted. It was Easter dinner, and it was one to remember. There were many people from so many countries that evening, and we all shared a prayer for a safe Camino.

During some introductions about where we were all from, I met a couple of German ladies that I was to repeatedly meet over the next few weeks.

Christina was tall, blonde, and cool. She always had a scarf tied and draped over her shoulder in true European cliche fashion and had done the Camino a few times already. She was loud and bubbly and could laugh and talk her way into and out of any situation. People gravitated towards her. The life force was strong in her!

Ingrid was her travel partner and was a polar opposite to Christina. She had long black hair, a quiet nature but a laugh that echoed down the Camino if she wanted to let it out.

They had met in Germany, as Ingrid had advertised for a walking partner for the Camino. She hadn't wanted to walk alone. So they'd practiced some short walks in Germany together to see if their pace matched and had dinners together to see if they could handle each other. I guess that did the trick because they were now Camino buddies.

It was an unforgettable night in Villar de Mazarife with old friends, new friends, and decisions to make.

PART II

THREADING-MIND
OVER BODY

19

A NEW COMMUNITY

VILLAR DE MAZARIFE TO HOSPITAL DE ORBIGO

There's a crack in everything, that's how the light gets in." – Leonard Cohen

· · ·

At a wonderful Hallelujah breakfast of scrambled eggs served by Pepe, we chatted to B. She was a young American lawyer from NYC who had just chucked that in and was now studying to become a doctor. That was another ten years of school! That's dedication!

She told her story of writing the MCAT test for medical school; she was allowed to take nothing in with her. As she passed through metal detectors, she had emptied her pockets. She had taken in 4 Halls lozenges with her because of a hacking cough. Each one was unwrapped, and the gloved security men examined them carefully. The lozenges were allowed into the room on a tissue like a delicate treasure. She jokingly told us that the security was worse than the test. Nevertheless, she had scored well and had been invited to enrol in a medical program. She was making a fresh start.

Then, she quietly told a few of us seated near her why she was walking the Camino. Her husband, also very young, had passed away, and they had often talked about doing the Camino together. She had decided to walk alone to help process her loss. She carried some of his ashes with her in a few empty bottles of nail polish. She planned to walk to Finisterre and sprinkle some of his remains in the ocean.

She joked a bit about the whole situation, but I could only imagine how difficult it all was. However, her ease with sharing her journey with us was inspiring.

Many other people I had met were walking to process grief. Walking, I knew, was an excellent way to clear your head and to make your body stronger. Walking also helped to give you the energy you move on and to see the possibilities of new beginnings. More and more, I also thought, that the Camino seemed to have underlying energy to it. Maybe it gave us all a reprieve from our busy lives and let us focus attention inwards. Even a simple walk around the block did this, but the focus of weeks of walking just did this on a much larger scale.

After breakfast, a few people were going to look at a telephone museum before starting the day's walk, and I decided to tag along.

Maeve and Lina decided not to go, and this seemed like a good point to say goodbye for a while.

"Well, Shannon," Lina said, "We walked a lot of kilometers together." She didn't talk a lot. This was mainly because she was a little self-conscious about her English. She shouldn't have worried though, her English was excellent, and I loved the German flavor of her spoken English.

"Yes, but I'll see you in Santiago. I feel like I am slowing both of you down." I was slowing them down, I knew. I walked carefully because of my blisters.

"Take care, Shannon," Maeve added. "I hope that you and your sister have a good walk together. I hope to see you again one day."

"Thank you so much, ladies. It has been wonderful sharing these days with you." I was meeting my sister in Sarria in about a week, and I was thankful to have this window of time to walk alone.

We gave each other big hugs and planned to meet in Santiago. We agreed to text each other and keep track of our progress. I strongly felt like I wanted to walk alone for a while.

I wasn't expecting much from the telephone museum, but I was pleasantly surprised. The owner had been a telephone lineman his entire career and had collected everything you could imagine related to telecommunications. He was very proud of it all (as he should have been) and wanted to show us everything. Every possible kind and color of phone was there, from princess phones to miniature British phone boxes. Receivers hung from walls, stacks of old phone books, phone lines, bells, and buttons; all were neatly organized in several rooms. We donated by making a deposit in an old phone box. Yes, communication was important!

It felt a little strange to be walking without Maeve and Lina, but soon I met a single Japanese girl traveling alone. She was only the 2nd Japanese person I had met here. She was from Osaka but worked in Ginza-an expensive area of Tokyo. This was her 2nd trip to do a section of the Camino. Next year, she planned to finish it. I spoke some Japanese with her since I had taught English in Japan for 13 years and still remembered a bit. We reverted to English soon. She did not appear to appreciate my Japanese pronunciation as much as I did.

We walked slowly together to Albergue Verde in the town of Hospital de Orbigo named after an old hospital on a river-bank. Many pilgrims of long ago, had walked through here on their way to Santiago, and had been able to use the hospital if they had been in need.

The Gothic, medieval, arched bridge crossed the Rio Orbigo here. As the story goes, a knight named Don Suero de Quinones was rejected by his one true love, and he put on an iron collar (a prisoner of love?) once a week to prove he couldn't escape from his feelings.

He also said that he would fight off 300 lances (a real Sir Lance-a-lot!) from any knights brave enough to joust with him on the bridge. Luckily for him, nine friends came to help, and weekly jousting matches were watched by spectators. He didn't get to 300; it was closer to 200, but he was declared the winner. His iron collar was ceremoniously taken off, and he was sent on a pilgrimage to Santiago. It must have been a bit like an early reality show, as he fought all those other knights for his true love.

The Japanese girl and I had a drink together at a pricey bar overlooking the river where the jousting match had occurred. It was a real Spamalot moment and a nice place to sit and imagine the knights jousting there long ago.

We got to Albergue Verde later in the afternoon, and I loved it instantly. There was a bit of a hippy vibe here, with large cushions spread out on the floor to relax on and guitars available for use. Incense hung in the air, and you could help yourself to herbal tea. (Though, all-you-can- drink tea did not quite have the allure of all-you-can-drink alcohol.) Massage and yoga were offered by donation, and hammocks were strung up outside around a great vegetable garden. It was a nice place to wind down after a long day of walking.

One of the best things was the shower here; there were massaging shower heads with plenty of hot water and even small stools to put your clothes on so they didn't fall off a hook onto the floor. It's the little things.

There was no sign of Angelina or Tomasso, though. I asked the owner, and he said Angelina was expected any day. I was disappointed. I didn't have any contact information for either of them and maybe I would never even see them again.

A bit sad, I hung out laundry, went to a large grocery store, and just chilled for a day. Then, I signed up for the communal dinner here, which wasn't until 8.

Just before dinner, Christina and Ingrid struggled in. They were both dealing with coughs and fatigue like me.

"I have my house on my back," said Christina. "I have everything I need and want for this Camino life. It's like being sick at home!"

The dinner was terrific. The albergue hospitaleros played some energetic music on guitars for us. It was a delicious vegetarian dinner with salads, soups, bread, hummus, and a lot of wine. Everything was fresh and homemade. There was an amazing communal feeling around a small table of international pilgrims as we dined by candlelight. Pilgrims from England, Germany, Italy, Slovenia, Scotland, Japan, and Canada were in the house!

Christina was a bit overcome with emotion at how lovely the night was, and it was indeed one of those incredible travel moments. A lady from Sacramento had a birthday, and we all got a large slice of chocolate cake. The lights had been dimmed further, and a hospitalero made a speech about living in the moment and not in the past or the future. We finished off the night listening to some Enya music and humming along together.

I could see why Angelina thought that it was such a special place. It felt like a magical spiritual retreat, another stepping stone on the way to Santiago.

20

A CAMINO BUG

HOSPITAL DE ORBIGO TO ASTORGA-15 KM

"The compact between writing and walking is almost as old as literature -- a walk is only a step away from a story, and every path tells." - Robert Macfarlane

After Hospital de Orbigo, it was a pleasant stroll into a small town with no jousting, but there was some hoisting of a coffee cup. This stop was necessary as it was a little cooler this morning. Also, I was walking completely alone, and it felt great!

Just before Astorga, in the middle of nowhere, a small oasis appeared on the dusty red earth called Casa de Los Dioses. It was a tiny pilgrim abode where you could help yourself to fruit, snacks, or drinks and make a donation. Bananas, apples, and watermelon were positioned across an open space. It was evident that this place was built with love and trust. With hammocks, a stone circle, and fabulous decor and shelter, it was a great place to stop for a breather. It felt warm and welcoming, which I think everyone who stopped here loved.

Of course, I found the Germans inside.

"We have been waiting for you! Have some tea and warm up. This is David's place. He was here for over seven years caring for pilgrims, and then he decided to go away. He got tired of the tourists; not enough true pilgrims for him anymore. It is amazing that he has come back to care for us all again," Christina told me.

"That's so cool," I said. But how did Christina know everything all the time?

What a kind and gracious person David must be. This tourist vs. pilgrim dilemma was something that I had been pondering. It was true that I was on an old pilgrimage route, but was I a pilgrim? I didn't think so. Of course, some things were difficult, but I felt more like I was on a great hike than a spiritual journey that a true pilgrim should be on. Perhaps I would feel different in Santiago.

"David had struggles in his life. Walking helped him so much. He has walked the Camino barefoot."

David was like so many unique people helping all of us get to our destination. That was part of the magic of it all.

It was still a little cool, and we huddled in a little shelter, warmed by a wood-burning fire, slowly sipping our tea for quite a while. David came inside (barefoot, I noticed) and sat with us for a while. We chatted a bit about the road that day, but mostly we just sat enjoying the warmth inside. When a new group of pilgrims arrived, David went out to the stand to help them.

Eventually, we decided that we had better keep moving. I grabbed a banana for the road, put a donation in his box, shouldered my pack, and I was off. I told Christina and Ingrid that I would see them later.

I'd been fighting the cold and cough that everyone had and had a relatively easy day. I was sucking on honey sticks, drinking liters of water, and crunching on cough candies. I wasn't getting any better, though. I was done by the time I got to Astorga just after lunch. I just wanted to check into the first hotel I could find and have a room to myself for the first time in 19 days.

However, I could not find one! All the hotels I wanted to check into were closed. I'd already walked past an albergue, and I didn't feel like walking back. I couldn't call any more hotels since my phone was dead now, too. I was close to tears; how pathetic! I wanted to be someplace warm, snuggled in bed, and get over this cold.

I found the tourist office and got a map, and managed to find two more hotels that were recommended. However, they both didn't open till 2 pm. So I kept trudging on and found a grocery store. I bought some orange juice, chocolate and more tissues and sat down on a bench in a bit of park and continued to feel sorry for myself.

After a bit of a break I felt a bit better, and I walked

around and stared at Gaudi's palace and cathedral in the driz-zle. I'd read that Astorga was the chocolate capital of Spain, and I noticed that every shop window seemed to be displaying boxes of chocolate. But I didn't care if Willy Wonka himself showed up; I needed to get out of the rain.

Somehow I found another hostel; it was the only place that was nearby, open, and not astronomically expensive. It was the albergue San Javier.

I hadn't wanted to stay in a dorm and keep everyone up with my coughing, but I needed to get off the streets. I was thrilled I found this place. It was friendly, had a lovely fireplace and kitchen area and was managed by an older guy named Marty, who liked to talk quite a bit. He told me he had done the Camino 27 times, had survived a heart attack, had the last rites administered, but had eventually recovered.

He had started to walk short distances when he could, and eventually had gotten stronger. He accredited his recovery and health to the Camino. Now to give back, he volunteered his time helping out here.

"I'm a bit sick." I told him after he'd stamped my pilgrim credential, "Are there any dorms that are empty?"

"I'll put you with the other sick ones. Everyone seems to have a cold now. Try a shot of grappa, it will warm you and help too."

"I'll think about it," I said, and walked up the old steps to find my room. It had been a monastery once, and the old wooden floors were well-worn and creaked with every step. I was glad to see that there were only a few other bags in the room.

I needed to wash clothes here, and I used the sinks in the courtyard. Some pilgrims sat around soaking their feet in pans of water. I might have enjoyed pounding my clothes down and up and beating the dust out of them, but I was feeling too run down. So I gave them a few half-hearted slaps and hung them on some washing lines.

I was just going back upstairs when big gooey drops of rain fell, and I wanted to stretch my arms up and yell, "Are you kidding me!" but I didn't.

Instead, I grabbed the dripping clothes, draped them upstairs over radiators, and hoped they would dry by morning. Since I was already sort of wet by now, I decided to have a shower.

The showers here were not ideal. I had to keep whacking the tap to keep the water flowing. I seemed to get about 10 seconds of water at a time before it cut off. Each time the water restarted, it took a few seconds to heat up. With one hand shampooing my head and the other hand angrily smacking the tap, it took a lot of concentration, commitment, and anger management to get through that shower.

I'd found in some places that the Spanish toilets were a bit problematic too. Yes, when you flipped a switch, the lights came on. But then, when you least expected it, the lights could cut off to save energy. All I can say is that you'd better know where the toilet paper was located! It can take some time jumping around or waving your arms to trigger the lights to come on again.

Of course, this water and energy efficiency is a good thing. But, unfortunately, it doesn't happen in North America, but because I was still feeling sick, I did not enjoy that energy saving shower experience.

Feeling hungry and sorry for myself, I wandered the streets again a bit later, coughing and looking for food. Unfortunately, every restaurant was closed nearby; it was siesta time. I didn't feel like exploring much, so I ended up at another small grocery store where I just bought a can of baked beans and a hunk of bread. I cooked that up in the small kitchen, practically licked the platter clean, washed the dishes, and then sat by the fire for a bit.

Everyone seemed to be in their groups here, and I think also I was not feeling very social.

I went off to bed early and decided against the grappa shots. Instead, I enjoyed swigging from my bottle of yummy cherry cough syrup through the night. I'm pretty confident that helped me sleep a lot too!

I was surrounded in the dorm by an Australians couple from Melbourne and an Italian guy and a Brazilian girl who were also sick. They all told me they'd accompany me for that shot of the local grappa alcohol if I got tired of my cough syrup. How very kind and considerate of them all!

There was no sign of bedbugs here for me, though some people had advised me to repeatedly check the bed in Astorga. However, we were all given a thick woolen blanket, and I suppose that could have been a good reservoir for the bedbugs.

I was fortunate that I never came across them (and they didn't come across me!) at all. But I don't think that I would have been affected too badly. However, some people are very allergic and have horrible reactions.

If you did ever come across bed bugs, you needed to wash all your clothes in extremely hot water and dry them as soon as possible. Heat killed them. Many people also put their backpacks inside a large garbage bag and left them out in the sun if the weather cooperated. Pilgrims, unfortunately, carried the bed bugs from albergue to albergue sometimes. I hoped I never gave one a lift on my backpack from anywhere!

There was whispered talk of wolves, bandits, and a snowstorm in the bunks tonight. I wanted the weather to be brighter in the morning! My Camino fire was still keeping me warm, and I hoped the only Camino 'bug' I had was the desire to keep on walking to Santiago!

21

FINDING FONCEBADON

ASTORGA TO FONCEBADON-25KM

" The trail is the thing, not the end of the trail. Travel too fast and you'll miss all you are traveling for."-Louis L'Amour

What a day! I set off at 7 am, feeling very tired because the Italian guy, a Brazilian girl, and I were coughing all night. I felt terrible for the other healthy people in the room. I was hoping I wouldn't meet the Aussies from the dorm ever again. However, I met them all at the first open cafe about an hour later. Awkward! They seemed fine with being kept awake all night from my coughing, but were they? I felt so bad!

There was a little rain, then snow flurries by the time I was walking out of town. At my second stop for a coffee, I met Christina and Ingrid, and a couple of American missionaries huddled around a fire. Boy, did they have some stories about the other albergue I didn't stay at.

At the other place, which shall remain nameless, the manager would not give out extra blankets (their sleeping bags were not warm enough!), and people hadn't been able to sleep because they'd been so cold.

As if that wasn't enough, there was some tacky, hanky panky on the upper bunk above Christina. So, with all that creaking, there had not been much sleep for anyone last night! There were going to be a lot of grumpy pilgrims on the road this day.

I made a pit stop at the Cowboy Bar in El Ganso, an iconic place to get a coffee or something more substantial. A few guys were sitting at the bar with their backs turned. Two other older Spanish men, complete with cowboy hats, were picking some banjos when I moseyed in. The echoing twang must have brought an ache to one young American guy who'd just walked in too.

"Let me play you a Southern song!" he said rather aggressively as he grabbed a spare banjo out of its case and began to position his fingers.

Well, he should have known that the first rule of Cowboy Bar Fight Club is never grab another musician's banjo.

So, just as young Clint Eastwood was getting ready to strum a tune, possibly the song from the film "Deliverance" (but we'll never know for sure), the banjo's owner jumped up angrily from his comfortable stool at the bar.

"Don't touch my banjo!" he shouted and glared at the young American.

The American must have seen something scary in those not-lying Spanish eyes since he quickly placed the banjo back in its case, mumbled "sorry," and walked on out the bar without even getting a Sasparilla.

The other banjo players had continued to play without missing a beat, or at least a chord. I bought an Aquarius at the bar since the action was done. Mainly I bought it so I could use the toilet out the back. A sign stated as much.

Chugging my Aquarius, I noticed the place was covered with old souvenirs like license plates, hats, flags, horns, and used bullets, even an old pinball machine. The guy behind the counter, who looked like an actor from a Spaghetti Western (or was it a Paella Western in Spain?), wore a cowboy hat and boots, was not friendly, and did not welcome any photos. In other words, a real cowboy!

Perhaps I should have slammed my Aquarius down on the bar and shouted, "Give me another!" but I was a little scared of him. So I left the dueling banjos behind me (sadly, no swinging saloon doors to push open) and decided to take my chances outside.

I continued up the valley, crossing over streams, and walked through woods as the path climbed higher. I noticed the crosses pilgrims had tied to the fence, which made me stop for a second and pause and wonder about all the pilgrims who had taken the time to stop here.

I had planned to stop in Rabanal after walking about 20 km, but the rain was stopping, and the sun was shining, so I went another 7 km. I had some hot soup in Rabanal, though. It was a lovely picture-perfect medieval town; it had a real Bohemian vibe, I thought. There was Gregorian chanting here in the evenings. A Camino experience not to be missed, I was told, but I missed it.

Slowly, I saw Foncebadon in the distance, a scattering of crumbling stone buildings clinging to the hillside. Not exactly picture perfect. Most of the old buildings had caved in and collapsed, and there seemed to be few restaurants and shops. It looked bleak but pretty in the gathering mist, with grey slate and a spattering of some purple heather. The weather closed in around me and turned into a rainstorm just as I walked down the muddy track.

Foncebadon was a strange little place, somewhat cloaked in an air of melancholy. It seemed very real, though, and I hoped it never changed into a perfect town. I could even hear dogs howling and barking along with the wind. I remembered reading about large wild dogs here that had bothered some pilgrims years before.

According to the guidebook, this "mountain hamlet is now stirring back to life with the reawakening of the Camino." Hopefully, it would not stir too far.

I got a room at Convento de Foncebadon, which was very clean with a great restaurant and a Pilgrim's Meal option.

I loved staying in this old convent with its creaky wooden floors and artfully positioned old crucifixes and crosses on walls. There was an old motorcycle resting inside the restaurant, which I heard the owner used to race. It was an eclectic place for a very unique town. And, to make things perfect, who did I find in the restaurant in time to share dinner with - yes, my 2 German ladies!

"This town is my Camino diamond town," said Ingrid. "It is not perfect; it is rough like some diamonds."

"Before, a Roman road ran through here; it was a busy

place. But, another road was built around it, and it went down hill."

"Yes, I read that too. And, I read that in the '90s, only a mother and son lived here. Everyone else left to find work, I guess," I said.

"It is starting to breathe again a little," said Christina. "This is my third time in this town. Every time Foncebadon is a little stronger, a little more alive. Can you understand my simple English?"

"Yes, Christina, very, very well."

We all went to sleep early, and I enjoyed swigging cough medicine without having to worry about bothering any other pilgrims. I even enjoyed a little Spanish SpongeBob Square-Pants on TV to lull me to sleep. I needed to get rid of my cold, and a bit of self-care was definitely in order.

22

A CROSS TO THE LAST TEMPLAR KNIGHT

FONCEBADON TO MOLINASECA-20KM

"I took the one less traveled by, And that has made all the difference."–
Robert Frost

In the morning, Foncebadon had changed quite a bit. Out of
the window of my room, I saw a white blanket spread over the
town. It covered the collapsed roofs of houses, piles of old
timber, the hanging chimneys, and rough yellow gorse. On the
road, it had melted, and here and there, large muddy puddles
had formed already from the melting snow.

The snow swirled and glittered on the thorny bushes of
lilac and yellow as I walked out of town. They looked beautiful this morning. There was no one in sight yet this morning,
as my muddy black shoes squelched through puddles of
melting snow and my poles plunged into the brown earth.

I trekked as far as the Cruz de Ferro- the iconic symbol of
this pilgrimage. It's believed that some cross had been here
since Roman days. Perhaps it was once a kind of guidance
marker for pilgrims in lousy weather. Now it was represented
by a cross on top of a tall wooden pole sitting on a huge
mound of stones.

It was a custom for pilgrims to leave a stone here that
symbolized grief, sadness, or thankfulness. The stone would be
there forever; the feeling might not.

I had a small green stone I had picked up in Leon. The
story was embarrassing. Leaving the Franciscan albergue in
Leon, a bowl of mints was sitting on the desk when we
checked out. I helped myself and popped one into my mouth
on leaving reception (I'm not sure who was more surprised,
me or the guy on the desk). It didn't taste like a mint cause it
wasn't; it was a decorative stone! I ended up spitting it into my
hand and then into a pocket in the side of my bag.

I had forgotten about the stone but had noticed it again
when I had been rummaging through my side pocket for

something. I was glad I had something to put at the cross now. I placed it in the middle of the cairn with all the other stones.

I didn't feel bad about my 'mint' from Leon; it fit in just fine. I saw stones with names, some with messages and dates, large and small, some crystals, some stone glass from a beach. Was it wrong to leave something without significant meaning? I don't think so. For me, that stone represented that I had made it that far. Yes, I missed the spiritual experience of carrying a stone and leaving it in a place where so many thousands who preceded me had left their burdens, sins, or prayers behind. But that was okay with me.

My guidebook described the cross like this:

"Where the cross is now located is thought to have been initially an altar built to the Roman god Mercury, whereas some stories say that it is where the Celts worshiped; either way, the origins were pagan. The cross is believed to have been placed here in the 11th century by Gaucelmo.

Traditionally pilgrims have left a rock here, whether picked up along their journey or brought all the way from their homeland. Some of the stones that have been left here contain little messages to loved ones or the name of the pilgrim's hometown.

Ingrid and Christina walked up as I was walking down from the large pile of stones. We took a few photos, and then Ingrid laid her stone of thankfulness. She was in remission from leukemia and had been doing the entire Camino as a way to say thanks. For the whole of the walk, she told us, she had the stone in her jacket pocket where she could hold it and be reminded of God's protection and to feel grateful. The Cruz de Ferro had a great significance for her. We all shed a few tears together—an exceptional place.

I told them to walk on ahead. I was still moving relatively

slowly due to my cough, and I didn't want them to see me crying.

A few kilometres down the road, I saw what I initially thought was a pile of rubble with signs: 222 kilometers from Santiago, and 2475 kilometers from Rome. Finally, it seemed I had reached Manjarin, population 1.

Some wood planks had been nailed up around some old stone walls, but many open gaps let the cold wind in. Flea-bitten dogs sat on their skinny haunches, shivering. Cute, dirty kittens roamed around mewing and huddling together, shaking to remove the fleas as they walked across tabletops and chairs.

I poured myself some hot water and added a spoon of instant coffee into a cup. I didn't want to consider the cleanliness of the place. I was glad that I'd my hepatitis shot back home. I needed something to warm up with, though. I dropped a donation into a metal box sitting on a dirty old table through a slot in the top. I helped myself to a biscuit, too; if I was going to live dangerously, I might as well go all the way.

According to posted papers on the walls, this was a donativo/albergue run by Tomas, who traced his lineage back to the Templar Knights. Trinkets like shells and crosses were for sale. Tomas himself reminded me of a tired, over-weight, grey-haired version of Captain Jack Sparrow from *Pirates of the Caribbean*, who had really let himself go. He wore a kind of tunic with a large Crusader-like cross stitched across the chest, a flowing cape, and a sword at his side.

Flute and what sounded like bagpipe music were coming from a damaged speaker that sat behind a counter. The whole place reminded me of a poorly run gift shop at a Renaissance Faire. All that was missing were fair maidens in long velvet gowns. It definitely felt a bit Medieval in that room.

Who didn't want to be drawn back to the time of the Templar Knights and perhaps experience what an actual

Pilgrim hotel felt like? Cleanliness was conspicuously absent here. It appeared Tomas made due from donations.

The government had tried to shut him down many times, but, he was still standing in his albergue, like a captain going down with his ship. He wanted to show people what it is like to be a genuine pilgrim, I suppose; maybe he was a little nuts, but I think he truly wanted to help pilgrims.

Perhaps Tomas embodied the true spirit of a modern-day knight. He hosted thousands of pilgrims, as did the Knights Templar, feeding and protecting them. Maybe he was what knights looed like now; middle-aged, gray-haired, with yellowed teeth—but still determined, proud, and loyal to the pilgrims of the Camino. An aging Captain Jack, still with a crew of some pilgrims who liked what he represented.

Tomas's treasure of the Templars on display included some old paintings, carvings, rusty swords, and a collection of scallop shells. Was there a real treasure hidden there somewhere?

What if Tomas was right? Pilgrims only needed the basics if they were true pilgrims. Perhaps somewhere in the back was a round table that was still meaningful. Crazy is just a matter of who's telling the story.

As I was finishing my coffee, Christina and Ingrid walked in.

"This place is so bizarre," I said.

"I stayed here once on my first Camino," Christina said quietly. "I will never sleep here again. The dormitory is in another building next door. You must sleep upstairs in the attic. Everything is dirty, and there are bugs. There is no water and just a hole in the ground to shit in. I was very sick after I left."

"I guess some people want this experience. But, it is a little too dirty for me too."

I got a stamp in my pilgrim passport; Christina and Ingrid didn't bother.

From here, it was a very, very steep downhill to El Acebo; my legs moaned quietly. I got lunch at a new albergue run by a guy from Texas. The entire morning was rather snowy, rainy, and cold, so it was nice to warm up along the way. He had a big pot of chili cooking that tasted great. It was a much cleaner place than Tomas's albergue. But, this was just my opinion. It depended on what you were looking for.

The path was brutal after this stop, too. More downhill on loose rocks. People were sometimes racing down. Were they nuts? On roads or larger paths, I could care less about how you did your Camino, but navigating a steep slope on narrow rocky paths was not the time to prove how tough you are. Some guy blew out his knee, and I passed one woman being consoled by her friends. It was survival of the fittest for all of us that day.

I was pretty careful and arrived downhill in one piece, past the chestnut grove. This freaky little ditty was in the guidebook.

'Up the airy mountain, down the rushy glen, we daren't go a hunting, for fear of little men," that's a little weird, right?

What little men? I hadn't spotted anything unusual. Were they hiding and lurking somewhere?

Later in the afternoon, the roofs of Molinaseca came into sight, and the final approach was over an old stone bridge. I guessed I was finally past the little men.

I decided to avoid the dorm one more night. It was only 30 euros for a single room at El Capricho de Josana. It seemed very new and had a wonderful restaurant and even a bathtub and hairdryer. Best of all, it was warm.

My legs were aching this day, and it was a shame that I

couldn't change my legs like car tires for winter or summer. I could have used some new ones.

This was a super small town, and it seemed nothing was open till 7:30. I had arrived before it really started chucking down.

23

DOG DAYS

MOLINASECA TO CACABELOS-23KM

"Only those who risk going too far can possibly find out how far they can go." – T. S. Eliot

Another late start—about 8 am. I decided to see how far I could go until my legs got really tired. I seemed to hit a wall at 25 km and don't think I could have walked any further.

As I walked out past Molinaseca about 8:30- the Camino went past a school bus stop with lots of elementary school kids in uniforms lined up to get on the bus with their parents waiting. I had to wait a bit to cut through them, and this little boy said 'Buen Camino,' which I heard 50 times a day as I passed through towns or met other pilgrims. But, then the little boy also said, 'Country'? (in English) I said, 'Canada.'

His dad stopped me and said his son loved the 'peregrinos' and had a list at home of all the pilgrims' countries. The kid had also learned other English words like 'Have a good walk! 'I heard him say that as I walked off.

I thought this was cool - imagine all the different kinds of people with backpacks that little boy saw every single day! Perhaps he will be a peregrino one day himself!

The road wound along some urban sprawl today into Ponferrada; a charming medieval town with many quaint cafes and squares. I had a coffee with a French girl near the river, who I had met before in Astorga. We both agreed that we had loved the past few days. Even the snow.

This town was famous for the best-preserved Templar castle in Spain, originally 13th century. I just saw the outside, and I was still impressed! The Templars had become power-ful, wealthy, and political men, and that castle with its turrets and thick walls looked like something out of an old movie. I didn't go in as I was passing through town, but I heard there was a great collection of beautiful antique books. Perhaps there are a few mysteries to be found within those pages. The real location of the Holy Grail?

Then I got lost somewhere in the winding narrow Ponferrada. I couldn't find any more of the ubiquitous yellow arrows anywhere, and had to ask for directions. I got back on track, eventually. It's a big place! I don't love these big towns, as it is hard to find the markers always.

The weather truly sucked all morning: wind and rain. But foul weather meant I met Fido, the incredible Camino canine. (Pronounced Fee-do because he was a French pilgrim doggy.) He seemed to be a mixed breed of some kind of small terrier.

Fee-do had walked from Burgos, which was about 180 miles. He had a cute little yellow raincoat and walked 10 miles maximum a day I found out. He was so cute, but I thought it must have been a little challenging for the two people walking with him. I noticed that Fee-do stopped to sniff things a lot.

It had been drizzling all morning, and I kept passing Fee-do and the two people in their red or blue ponchos. They looked like giant turtles, struggling forward, not giving up.

We all stopped together in a coffee shop, when the rain got too heavy. They removed their tortoise shells, introduced themselves and said they were from France.

"What brings you guys to the Camino?" I ventured.

"We are both old school friends, recently divorced, trying to sort out our lives. I left my cats at home with my ex-, but I don't want to become a cat-lady. I need to change my life. Start a new job, maybe."

"I'm happy being a dog lady, though," her friend laughed.

"Is it hard walking with Fee-do?" I asked.

"No, it is a pleasure. Everyone wants to talk to us and to meet Fee-do. Yes, he is slow, but he lets us see things with fresh eyes. It is a different view of the Camino. We call him our special 'perro-grino!'"

"Haha, I loved that pun on the Spanish word for dog, which was 'perro.' How many people had made that joke over the years, thousands or millions?

"Is it hard to find a place to stay? I know some albergues don't accept dogs."

"Yes, it is true. But, we have booked in advance at places that will be happy to have Fee-do. We both feel a little safer with him too."

What an incredible experience, I thought. Walking the Camino with man's best friend. And what an adventure for Fee-do. How many dogs get to go on such a canine Camino!

We finished our coffees and were happy to find that the rain had let up a bit and we put our raincoats away. I walked with them for a bit and then continued as Fee-do was sniffing at some flowers on the side of the road. What amazing smells he must pick up everywhere. I wondered, though, if he spent some time in the evenings licking his paws like exhausted pilgrims did rubbing their feet.

It was nice to see this friendly dog today, as I had been a little afraid of dogs on the Camino. I had read of pilgrims being attacked and people carrying big sticks to ward them off. At least I had my trekking poles. Maybe these stories were just the embodiment of our fear of the unknown on the Camino. I don't know, but I continued to walk gingerly and carry my sticks in the small towns when the growling dogs sometimes approached.

I passed through a couple of other small towns - but there were not many places to stop today. Finally, in the last hour, the sun broke through, and I found myself in a lovely forest. A guy had set up a trailer and made smoothies and sold home-made cake at his place called La Siesta. It was a good excuse for a break. He told he had to rent the space, pay taxes, and just barely made enough to live on. It couldn't have been much - oh, and he'd walked the Camino nine times.

When I reached Camponaraya, I found a place with a sign that said, "Pilgrim Stop. Wine and *pintxos* tasting. 1.50 euros."

A little wine and a little snack were exactly what I needed for the final push.

I floated into Cacabelos and found an albergue called Santa Maria, and I may even have found a little more wine there!

24

GONE FISHING

MOLINISECA TO AMBASMESTAS 27 KM

"If you are in a bad mood, go for a walk. If you are still in a bad mood, go for another walk"-Hippocrates

. . .

Yay!! The sun came out again! It was another beautiful walk this morning past vineyards and through a couple of small towns. The town of Villa Franco looked gorgeous, but I had to keep going, as I had a long walk this day.

Not a lot going on today except walking, walking, walking. I had planned to go further, but I kept seeing signs for a Pescadero (Spanish for fish farm) Albergue. So I stopped, and my feet were glad I did. It was owned by a super friendly couple. My guess was the husband liked fishing.

The location was sweet. Hammocks were strung between a few trees, and all around, we were surrounded by lush green fields. A path meandered around a pond stocked with fish, and a few log cabins were constructed around the water. It had the feel of a rustic, comfortable fishing get-away.

We had a choice of catching our dinner or enjoying pre-caught. I opted for pre-caught. The menu was to be home-made pumpkin soup, fish and salad, and dessert. Behind the cabins was a large vegetable garden. It would be great to have some healthy food. No rubbery chicken tonight!

I found out the owners were from Russia. They had tried many locations in the world, from Costa Rica to Malaysia. Finally, they chose Spain and had been here three years enjoying the life and space they had chosen.

I was back in a dorm room, but I was pretty happy that no one else had showed up. I had the entire 12 bed dorm all to myself! I guessed that other people decided to walk to the top of the hill.

I sat outside on a little verandah blogging a little and met Pat and her husband, Dennis. It turned out that they were from Washington State but frequently visited my neck of the woods-San Jose.

She was a psychologist, and it was interesting to hear her perspective on the Camino. In addition, she was collecting data for a book she was writing about relationships on the walk.

I told her a bit about my experience and walking together with Maeve and Lina, and then feeling like I wanted to walk alone for a while. She was a good listener, but her "ahs," and "mms," and head-nodding really did make me feel like I was in therapy on the Camino. Was I?

"Why are you here, Shannon?"

"I just want to walk. Hmm, why are you here," I countered.

"What do you think?" God, she really was a psychologist.

"I guess," I began, "we are here for these conversations, for these connections, and relationships we find. It's hard to find these moments at home."

It was tough to talk to her while she scribbled notes in a book.

"People open up on the Camino," she said without looking up. "It's because they are often looking for a change. As a result, they get stronger; they lose their fear."

"Is that what your book is about?"

"Some of it. But it's also a bit personal. Dennis and I have done two other Caminos, and we have learned a lot we want to share."

"Oh, like what?"

"Well, that's for the book."

We sat for a bit longer (with Pat not sharing much about herself. How very psychological of her!), and then Dennis sat with us too. He was reading a book and saying little. He didn't seem like a big talker- I thought I knew why.

A few other people walking the Camino passed by the albergue but decided not to stay. I could understand their hesitation, since there really was nothing here. (Except for Pat scribbling in her little notebook and me sweating bullets over her line of questioning). Nobody else stopped, so I'd have the big dorm room to myself. Yay!

We could see the fish swimming around in the small algae-covered pond, occasionally splashing and catching a bit of air. I wasn't sure how keen I was on eating these fish anymore.

But, the dinner, with a fat friendly cat also observing us eat around some fish bones, was quiet. As I'd expected, it was also delicious.

After dinner, we talked of our experiences on the Camino. With Dennis there, I was a little relieved that Pat had no more deep-diving questions for me. They had also loved Leon; it seemed we had that in common at least.

The Russian owners had a unique idea at this albergue. After dinner, many pieces of paper were placed into a glass in the middle of the table. Dennis, Pat and I reached in and chose a piece of paper. Each note had an inspirational quote on it.

Mine said: 'Above all, do not lose your desire to walk.'

I loved it. Dennis and Pat also loved their quotes which of course related to walking too. I saw Pat saving them in her notebook. Maybe they would make it into the book?

Despite my nagging disappointment at not hearing any of Pat's stories, I know we all went to bed feeling lucky to have stayed at this beautiful place and very inspired to walk in the morning.

It was nice to hear the sound of water running outside, birds chirping, and cows mooing, and then nothing but silence.

25

MIDDLE KINGDOM

AMBASMESTES TO O CEBREIRO -15 KM

"Not all those who wander are lost." – J.R.R Tolkien

In the morning, Pat and Dennis were long gone by the time I started. I found this day tougher than Day 1 when I was running on adrenaline, I guess. I started having flashbacks about that first day over the Pyrenees, but I talked myself down off a ledge without anyone noticing. I mean, I was told it was only 10 kilometers from Ambasmestes. I didn't realize that was a 4 hour all UPHILL walk over small rocky trails! I did a lot of swearing! It seemed to help!

Brierley's book had the elevation gains included in it every day, so you knew how difficult the day might be. I tried not to worry about this. But, this day I peeked, (as well as peaked!) and knew that it would be pretty tough going. I didn't realize how tough. Plus, I had my pack.

I passed through the town of Las Herrerías early in the day. I'd seen a few signs advertising horses for 35 euros to the top. I was planning on that option. But, when I reached the town and the albergue there was no one there. They must have already done their "Hi Ho Silvers Away" and were off hooves over rocks up up and away. I think you would need to stay overnight there to sort the horsepower thing out. Look for signs advertising Al Paso in Las Herrerias, and contact Victor about his horses.

I'm glad I walked up. It was pretty challenging, but the views were amazing! The uphill trudge went on for hours.

About halfway up, there was a little town called La Faba where I had an icy cola and a basket of potato chips. It kept me going until finally I was climbing into O Cebreiro, just after a boundary marker for the Galician region of Spain. It was so green it reminded me so much of Ireland. It felt like I had climbed into an Asterix and Obelisk moment as the muddy path became neat cobblestones. I had to stop for a second to soak it all in.

The buildings were made of slate and other stone; some were conical shaped (these were called *paloozas*; now preserved homes that showed how people had once lived up on the mountain top), and the smell of wood fires permeated the air. Or was it a Lord of the Rings alternate universe? Was I in the

Land of Middle Earth? I hoped that creepy Gollum character wasn't around anyplace.

It was naturally Neolithic here! On all sides, the land swooped down, making it a natural pilgrim's rest from the earliest days and honestly like a portal to another realm. I could see all the mountains of Galicia spread out behind me.

I resisted the urge to crawl down the cobblestones; I felt exhausted. But then, I spotted a bar across the only street. My Precious! I headed over!

I ordered a beer and asked for a single room. God, my Spanish was getting good! I figured I deserved a room, as the hostel wasn't open yet. The bar owner led me across the road to a building that seemed more like a family house than a hotel. But, the room on the second floor was perfect. I had my own bathroom. Tired and contented, I collapsed on the bed for a few hours.

I had instantly loved this magical, mythical place of O Cebreiro. Have you ever arrived someplace and felt like you had come home? That is how I felt when I crested into that town of only 4 or 5 hotels, two albergues, and a few restaurants, and of course the church. It was a village that had been in existence since ancient times.

I prefer small towns to cities, and this was a very small town. There was not a lot to do here except for eating or drinking, so if you passed through in the morning, it might not hold your attention. Nevertheless, I loved Galicia with its strong Celtic presence.

I loved the smell of O Cebreiro as much as I liked its look. It smelt like wood fires, horse manure, and old earth and green grass. The air was fresh and clean, but it was like sucking in the past when you inhaled.

It looked like maybe something out of a Tolkien tale. Celtic bagpipe music poured out from some small shops. There were also many monolithic burial mounds, and I suspected an earthy respect for the natural world here. I loved the unique buildings and different vibe here in this distinctively Celtic area.

There's a language here called 'Galego' still being preserved in poetry/lit and spoken by many locals. Historians believe that Gaelic people who spoke a Celtic dialect lived here since the bronze age. They must have been happy until the Romans came, but they would have had a hard time going up that damn mountain too!

I found a cool restaurant called Venta Celta, overlooking a ridge snuggled beside other slate-covered thatched-roof buildings. Above my head was an open ceiling of massive logs. They'd been here for a long time—strings of dried plants and onion bulbs dangled from nails. A fireplace in one corner blazed comfortingly. It was perfect.

A woman who had a face like wood carving came over with a menu from behind an open kitchen bar area. She scared me a little.

I ordered my first bowl of Caldo Gallego (a Galician soup with white beans, potatoes, and greens). It was steaming hot and just what I needed. There were few other people inside as it was mid-afternoon. I was lucky it was open as it was siesta time.

The soup warmed me up and was delicious. The woman stood behind the bar, stirring a large cauldron of soup and sometimes looking at me. She had probably stood in that same spot behind a counter for the 5o years serving coffee and beer.

I read my book a bit and saw the woman cut a piece of cake and bring it over to me.

"Gratis" (free), she said.

"Gracias," I said, a little surprised at her kind gesture.

I took a bite; it was a kind of carrot cake. "Deliciosa, I murmured."

She stood for a few seconds watching me eat and said something in Spanish I couldn't understand.

I said, "Hablo un poco de español." (I speak only a little Spanish)

She sighed. And I watched her walk back to her large battered pots of soup.

I sighed a little, too. It would have been amazing to have been able to talk to her. I sensed that she wanted to tell me something. Maybe even a secret of O Cebreiro. What might I have learned? I could tell from her face that she had a lot of stories to share. Language is such a path between cultures, and like the Camino, it can connect us all. Unfortunately, we had no language in common this day.

So, I could only finish the cake. A little while later, I wandered back to the bar where she stood waiting.

"Mucho gracias," I said, as I paid the bill.

She smiled and took both of my hands into hers and said several sentences very quickly while looking into my eyes. I have no idea what she said, but something passed between us. Again it might have been some ancient secret, or she could have simply been telling me, "Be certain that you don't eat at any other restaurants in town!" I guess I'll never know.

I wandered around some slightly tacky souvenir shops and then ended up at the same bar where I had got the room. A woman was speaking in Spanish at the bar. When she saw me walk in, she said, "Hello, so where are you from?"

"Canada."

"What? Wonderful! Me too! I don't meet that many Canadians here."

We shared some fries, some drinks, some laughs, and some memories of Canada. She was from Toronto, and I was originally from Winnipeg. I found out that she liked snow a lot more than I did.

She was also a founding member of a Canadian Pilgrims, Group, which was kind of neat. She'd done the Camino first in 1989 and had now lived near O Cebreiro for more than 20 years.

She told me how lucky I was to miss the storm. I had heard there was a white-out storm up here just three days ago. She was a lovely lady who does frequent lectures back home on the Camino but took the time to talk to me.

She also reminded me about the miracle that had happened in the town hundreds of years ago. One night, a fierce winter storm hit the village, and a priest assumed that no one would turn up. But a devout Christian man entered, and the priest was surprised and made fun of him by saying that it was not worth braving the storm just for a bit of bread and wine. The legend said that God turned the bread and wine into flesh and blood to punish the priest for his words and lack of faith.

This Holy Grail of O Cebreiro was not the same one used by Christ during the Last Supper. Still, the miracle was certified by the Pope!

"You must go into the church later and have a look at the Chalice. It made me shiver the first time I saw it," she told me.

"Of course," I said, very intrigued and excited. We talked for a bit longer, and then she was off back to her home. What must it be like to have lived there all of these years. From O Canada to O Cebreiro was a long way!

O Cebreiro was also where the resurgence of the Camino also began. The church is the final resting place of Father Elias Valiña Sampedro, who 'did so much in his lifetime to restore and preserve the integrity of the Camino,' according to Brierley. It was his idea to mark the Camino with the yellow arrows that now mark the way for hundreds of thousands of pilgrims every year.

In the misty evening, I went to mass in the church of Santa Maria, which is is one of the earliest surviving churches on the Camino, dating from the 9th century. Church bells played to let everyone know when to come. Parts of the service were in English, but the harmony and the acoustics in the church were exquisite. The best part was the blessing of the pilgrims. The pastor hugged everyone as we stood around the altar.

I even saw the Chalice on display here, but I especially loved a pilgrim's prayer that hung in that 9th-century church Santa Maria la Real. Fraydino, a Franciscan monk, wrote it. It sums up the Camino experience for me.

"Although I may have traveled all the roads, crossed mountains and valleys from East to West, if I have not discovered the freedom to be myself, I have arrived nowhere.

Although I may have shared all of my possessions with people of other languages and cultures, made friends with pilgrims of a thousand paths, or shared albergue with saints and princes, if I am not capable of forgiving my neighbor tomorrow, I have arrived nowhere.

Although I may have carried my pack from beginning to end and waited for every pilgrim in need of encouragement, or given my bed to one who arrived later than I, given my bottle of water in exchange for nothing; if upon returning to my home and work, I am not able to create brotherhood or to make happiness, peace, and unity, I have arrived nowhere.

Although I may have had food and water each day, and enjoyed a roof and shower every night; or may have had my injuries well attended, if I have not discovered in all that the love of God, I have arrived nowhere.

Although I may have seen all the monuments and
contemplated the best sunsets; although I may
have learned a greeting in every language or tasted
the clean water from every fountain; if I have not
discovered who is the author of so much free
beauty and so much peace, I have arrived
nowhere.

If from today I do not continue walking on your path,
searching a living according to what I have
learned; if from today I do not see in every person,
friend or foe, a companion on the Camino; if from
today I cannot recognize God, the God of Jesus of
Nazareth as the one God of my life, I have arrived
nowhere."

26

WALKING ON SUNSHINE

O CEBREIRO TO TRIACASTELA -21 KM

"Nothing great was ever achieved without enthusiasm." – Ralph Waldo Emerson

. . .

I woke up to a cold clear morning, and I could see my breath in the room. I had a nice view of the action below through my small window: there was not a lot, just a solitary pilgrim walking out of town. I dressed quickly; I was already wearing my pants and long sleeve shirt since it had been cold at night. I threw on my puffer jacket and walked back into the bar to leave the key attached to a worn piece of wood with the number 2 on it. It left a lovely echo in the empty bar.

No one was around as I hurried out of town in the direction of the lone walker I saw. It was misty, dark, calm, and silent. I glanced at my watch. It was 7:15 am. Where were all the other pilgrims? Had they already gone, or were they sleeping late? Had there been a Middle Kingdom event I'd missed? I thought it best just to keep moving.

The road continued on to a farmer's road; it narrowed to a small path. I just kept walking and saw no one. I had a power bar and an orange as I walked and still saw no one. Finally, I found a cafe and a few pilgrims wiping their milky cafe con leche off their chapped lips.

I ordered a coffee too, grabbed a plastic-wrapped, stale croissant, and looked around the room. I didn't recognize anyone, so I kept moving.

It was just a lovely walk up on top of the world-beautiful blue sky, green pastures, and the color of purple and yellow flowers everywhere. I passed through many farms and caught the delightful whiff of manure from time to time. I wished I was a horse for the rest of the walk and could have galloped through Galicia's green and pleasant land. All right, there were hills, but they were covered in majestic chestnut and oak and dotted with tiny hamlets. It was so darn picturesque.

How many people had walked these same paths? Was I walking in the same footsteps of soldiers, poets, thieves, scholars, Shirley MacLaine, and Paulo Coelho? There was so much history here, stories woven on top of one another, and I was now walking where the dead once stood. It was a place that makes you understand what it is to be alive. I felt very other-worldly up there.

I stopped a few more times for a coffee and got to Tria-castela early afternoon. It was a long plod. If yesterday was like visiting Ireland, today I felt like I was back in some rainy part of Yorkshire. Cows, chicken and goats had all come to say hello as I'd walked through the small towns.

Just before getting into Triacastela, was the famous chestnut tree. Apparently it was over 800 years old and had even been written about in the Codex. People, along with me, paused outside the tree and took a photo.

Triacastela meant' three castles,' and 3 Celtic castles used to surround the city. I didn't go looking for the ruins, just an albergue. I found Albergue Atrio, which I loved. There were beautifully preserved wood floors, stone walls, and an open plan concept, and it was so friendly for 10 euros. There was even a hairdryer available for use! I had lunch at the big restaurant Xacobea where all the pilgrims seemed to hang out.

I discovered that one of my dorm room residents, Linda, was also from San Jose, and I headed out to dinner with her and a few other people. She lived only a few streets away from me—but we had never met.

"Where do you go grocery shopping?" she asked.

"Trader Joe's and Safeway. How about you?" I added.

"Me, too! It's funny to think about San Jose, but I guess we have to start thinking about going home soon."

"I know; it seems so far away," I said, imaging the big grocery stores back home. I didn't recall seeing any white Spanish asparagus there. Going home? I hadn't even thought about it.

We forgot to exchange addresses, and I never saw Linda again. I look for her sometimes now when I'm out shopping, but we still haven't reconnected. Perhaps someday we will surprise each other in the fresh fruit and vegetable section at Safeway!

That night in Triacastela, I also heard about a young French guy I'd met who had been walking with a small dog. I heard that he had formally adopted the dog and planned on taking it back to France with him.

A Belgium lady's 93-year-old mother was being kept up to date on her daughter's daily progress. I saw a video of the mom taking her first steps out of a wheelchair in months wearing a sign that said, 'I can Camino too.' So cool!

A Kiwi woman had some good insight that has stayed with me.

"The Camino is like having a baby," she told us. "It is tough and tiring, but soon you will forget and want another."

I am not sure where she got that analogy from, but it seemed like it could be true. I had met a lot of people who had done multiple Caminos. The memories of those first Camino babies must have faded for them.

There was a different feeling at dinner. In our restaurant was also a busload of tourists, and we saw huge groups of cyclists in town. We were only one day away from Sarria, where many people started their Camino.

In Sarria, I would meet my sister. Since there would be two of us, we had booked rooms in advance on booking.com. This night was to be my last albergue experience. I stayed awake listening to the sounds of snoring, the creaking of bunk beds, the occasional cough, and savoring it all for the last time.

27

OLD FRIENDS

TRIACASTELA TO SARRIA-20 KM

"But the beauty is in the walking, we are betrayed by destinations." —
Gwyn Thomas

. . .

There were two ways to Sarria from here. One was longer and went via Samos (25 km), where one of the oldest monasteries still operates today. The other route was shorter (18 km) and went directly to Sarria. Thinking of Robert Frost yet again, I decided to take the shorter route to Sarria. Perhaps another time I would get to Samos.

The first part of the day was through another magical forest where I kept waiting to meet a hobbit. The scenery was lush with moss growing on tree trunks, ferns, gently rolling hills, and the ever-present cows! I kept meeting this guy all morning at coffee stops or just taking a rest. (He was too tall to be a hobbit!) I honestly thought that he was Dutch, but it turned out he was from Quebec! Guess my accent tracking radar was not working. He seemed like a nice Quebecois guy, but he walked too fast for me. "C'est la vie!"

After he left me in his dust, I walked in a large group of Koreans and Americans for a while. We were all very excited to be getting to Sarria. Most of them had started in Leon or Astorga. There were fewer and fewer people that had come all the way from St. Jean, I was noticing.

It was still a long walk into Sarria, and it went along a river with cute outdoor cafes for quite a while.

"Hey, Canada! Join us for lunch."

It was my German ladies; they had beat me to Sarria but had been struggling with illness and injury too. They both had the same Camino cough that I was dealing with, and Ingrid had a sore back.

I hadn't seen them since Foncebadon. Of course, that had only been five days ago, but it seemed like much longer. I could have walked together with them if I wanted, but I noticed I walked a lot slower than them.

"Where is the little sister?" Christina asked me.

"She's arriving tomorrow by train. I have to wash my clothes today to look cleaner!"

"Will she look like you without the dirt?" said Ingrid joking.

"No, she's blonde like Christina. They always look clean and have all the fun!" We laughed for a while together, excited to be in Sarria and to be nearer Santiago.

"What's it like walking into Santiago?" I asked Christina. I knew this was her third Camino.

"I still tingle just thinking about it. It is like someone will tickle me, and I can't stop feeling so happy. Is that the right English?"

"Perfect," I said.

They got up, wished me a 'Buen Camino', and I watched them walk down the street till their backpacks were out of sight. I promised to meet them in Santiago since I would be a few days behind them. I sat at that little table by the river for a long time, thinking about what was to come and about what had been.

I got a cheap hotel at the top of the steps into the older part of town, washed some clothes at a laundromat, went exploring, and sat down for a pilgrim's meal. Then, I just about spit out my white asparagus spear. Sitting just a few tables away, with her hand locked over another, and in intense conversation was Angelina! She was with Tomasso! It didn't look much like a mother and son lunch date!

Our eyes met, recognition flashed, and she removed her hand from on top of his. She gave me a late little smile. I could see that she was a little embarrassed. She whispered something to Tomasso, and he looked over, surprised too.

Well, this was awkward. But I waved, stood up, and walked over.

"My Shannon!" She stood up and hugged me, and Tomasso did the same.

"I thought we would never see you again. Sit, sit. We have much to discuss!"

Tomasso excused himself to go to the toilet. Well-played, Tomasso, well-played.

"Yes, it's true. I can see you know. We are in love!" Angelina excitedly exclaimed.

Well, she did seem happy and flushed. I was pleased for her. Though the age difference was huge, perhaps as much as 40 years. But did it matter?

"How did this happen?" I asked.

"At Hospital de Orbigo. We were late arriving because Tomasso's feet were so bad. We missed you, I know. We worked there for maybe one week, and love just happened."

"I'm so happy for you guys," I said. "So, what will you do now?"

"We are going to Santiago tomorrow. Tomasso must return home; his mother is ill."

"And you, what will you do?"

"I am going to Italy with him."

"Oh, that's wonderful," I said, now just about spitting out a little wine Angelina had poured for me. But, wow, I didn't see that coming.

Tomasso came back to the table limping a little. I wasn't the only one in Sarria with sore feet.

"You have told her?" he asked with a boyish smirk.

"I know, Tomasso! I'm so happy for you guys. The Camino provides!"

"It happened like magic. I have never felt a thing so powerful. I am excited for Angelina to meet my family. I have three brothers and one sister; they will love her."

They looked at each other frequently, smiling and enjoying their presence together. It was kind of cool!

"And, where are the other two, Lina and Maeve?" Angelina asked.

"I wanted to walk alone for a while," I said.

"We could see it," said Tomasso.

"Yes," said Angelina. "You were strong enough. The Camino cares for you now."

"Will you see them again?" asked Angelina.

"Of course, they are still a part of my Camino family." I will meet them in Santiago. My sister is arriving in Sarria tomorrow. I'm so excited about this too!"

"And, so you have one more journey, Shannon. It's time to look within. You have had physical and mental challenges. Now, it is time for your spirit."

"Do you believe all that is true?"

"I know it is true. I have experienced it all many times," she told me quietly.

"I have as well," said Tomasso, placing his hand over hers.

I felt like I was living in a movie moment. Had those two really met and connected, and were they going to fly off into the sunset on a Vueling Airlines flight? It was so surreal!

It was awkward now, sitting with the two of them, so I told them I was tired. Things were too different now to pretend they were the same.

We walked down the street for a while, and I wrote my address on a napkin. Unfortunately, neither of them had a cell phone. I was a little encouraged that Angelina folded up the napkin carefully and put it into her bag.

We hugged each other one last time, and I doubted that I would ever see or hear from either of them again. But, I would love to know how their story ended up.

I wasn't confident that Angelina would even get on that plane. But, if she did, she was tougher than I thought. It would take guts to meet Tomasso's family. But, I knew one thing, Maeve would be proud of her if she did. Angelina was not running away; she was running toward something.

PART III

HEADING-A NEW DIRECTION

28

THE SISTER ACT

DAY 28- STROLLING AROUND SARRIA

"There was never a pilgrim that did not come back to his own village with one less prejudice and one more idea." - Chateaubriand

. . .

171

In the morning, I moved to another hotel and met the loveliest lady, Marcella, who owned Casona de Sarria, another hotel, a dormitory, and an apartment- all for people who walk the Camino. Her entire family worked hard every day to maintain all the places, and I think it must have been hard to be friendly all the time, but she radiated positivity!

I had heard about this wonderful place from another pilgrim and was lucky to book a room since it was usually full. She was famous for providing a communal breakfast (with fruit and pancakes!) for anyone who wanted it. Usually, I would have toast, a croissant, or a banana for breakfast. Often, I just got up and walked to the first town without eating breakfast. It might be nice to have a little morning start-up coffee again. Marcella offered to drive over, pick us up, and take us to the breakfast location in her main hotel. What service!

I was shocked by the large number of places to stay and eat in Sarria. There was definitely a lot of competition here for pilgrim dollars. Albergues lined one of the main streets. Different restaurants offered more variety in food than I'd seen in quite a while. Restaurant chalkboards advertised bacon and eggs and steak dinners and drink specials. It was a whole new kind of Camino about to begin.

Sarria, I felt, was where all of us walking-weary warriors looking like crap in the clothes we had been wearing for four weeks, stared in shocked disbelief at all the neatly attired shiny people who were doing the last 100 km. Of course, they still needed to get stamps every day, but they would still get a pretty Compostela for doing the last 100 km. Perhaps I should have just done this?

You knew your battalion by the crinkled mud-streaked clothes, well-worn boots (or replacement sneakers from Decathlon), and people who were not setting a zippy little pace. There were many people like me on the path now, who had initially started in St Jean. They were the people with shin-splints, bandaged legs, and gashes in their heads walking the streets of Sarria. They weren't the ones stopping at every cafe to share a bottle of wine, tapas, and laughs. Instead, they were lying on bunks snoring by 9 pm.

When I looked at these laughing people in the cafes, I remembered near the beginning in Pamplona when I was doing that too. Oh, how things had changed!

I am glad I had the last week alone; I met so many great people and motivated myself to keep going and not rely on others to wait for me. It was nice to walk and think and get into a nice rhythm with the poles, the feet, and some tunes at times.

I was excited to be walking with my sister though for the last five days though. We would be splitting the cost of twin rooms, and it would be a lot quieter than in the albergues, as long as she didn't snore!

I had some time to kill before I met Sharlene's train, and I found myself staring this evening at a very sturdy-looking open beam, in my lovely Spanish room with its thick stone white-washed walls. I considered that the Camino experience was, at times, like a balancing act on an open beam. You had to keep walking and not fall off. Injuries, illness, frustration, exhaustion could all cause you to step off the Camino. For some people, it was the spiritual journey that kept them going and re-balanced their lives. For other people, it could be a combination of things—fitness, health, personal challenges, or perhaps the goal to reach the end in Santiago. You just had to stay on the beam.

Near dinner time, I went to meet down to Sarria station to meet the 'sista'! I had been texting with her the previous day, so I knew that she had arrived in Barcelona. But I had heard nothing from her since, so I hoped she had caught the correct train. Perhaps Wi-Fi was to blame. She was a little out of her comfort zone with this trip, though I knew that she could do anything she decided to do. I was lucky I had time to walk the whole Camino from St Jean. Unfortunately, many people did not have the luxury of time. So, the 100 km—the Camino-lite version was the chosen path. But it was worth it too.

The train did not arrive at the scheduled time. So I waited and waited some more. There was no sign of it, and there were very few people at the station Then, finally, I saw a train chugging down the track. That had to be it!

I watched as people got off, but I didn't see her. Then, way down the platform, I recognized a blue backpack she had purchased. She had made it!

She seemed pretty happy that I had actually shown up.

We walked together happily back to the hotel. I tried to see Sarria through her eyes. A small town that was not that quaint-looking near the station. There were a lot of nondescript office buildings and unpleasant-looking shops on the walk to the hotel. When we got to the older part of town, it looked much more picturesque with medieval style buildings, cobblestone streets, a few churches and a lot more people.

We had a dinner of pizza and wine and a little tiramisu to top things off, and decided to call it an early night. But on the way back to the hotel, I saw someone I knew coming out of the church as we strolled back to the hotel.

"Raymond!" I hadn't seen him in ages.

"Hi! Good to see you again," he said.

"This is my sister; she's just arrived."

"I still have lots of energy and nicely pressed clothes!" she joked.

"That won't last long!" he joked.

We talked for a bit and then planned to meet up in Portomarin the next day.

"Does that happen often? Running into people?" she asked.

"All the time. You keep running into the same people in different places all the time."

I couldn't imagine how she felt that first exciting night. But then, I remembered the feeling of butterflies in my stomach when I started from St Jean Pied de Port.

I knew that she must feel the same, and there was no better feeling in the world. It was the excitement of not knowing what the next day would bring. We were far away from our lives back home, with time to take it easy and to stop to look for butterflies if we wanted to.

29

STAIRWAY TO HEAVEN

DAY 29- SARRIA TO PORTOMARIN-23 KM

"The human body can only do so much. Then the heart and spirt must take over." - Sohn Kee-Chung

As promised, a car and driver arrived to take us to the main hotel for breakfast. It was Marcella's husband in a shiny red Mercedes convertible. Already I felt like I was about to experience a different kind of Camino. Maybe we should have asked for a lift to Santiago. We could have been there in under 2 hours!

The communal breakfast with PANCAKES, fruit, toast, juice, coffee, meats, and cheese was lovely. They did that every morning; what a lot of work! But what an excellent start to the Camino for so many people.

We shared a long breakfast table with some guys from Florida, a Danish couple, a South African Camino guru (who told me everyone gets sick in the middle of the Camino, and my final emotional part of the Camino was coming up. Hmmm.)

After breakfast, it was time to start and we excitedly followed the other walkers out of town. I used this strategy of following people a lot. This way, I didn't have to look for the yellow arrows on walls, pavement, or signs, as long as the people I was following were figuring it out. I hadn't got lost yet! More ominous music!

It was a perfect morning for walking and the crowds thinned out as we got away from the city. The sisters were off!

Some of the morning, we walked with Luigi from Italy and Canadian Ken. They were like barbie doll men; tall, handsome young men with sensible haircuts and long flexible legs who shared some of their journey with us but soon left us in their dust! We never saw them again. That's how it usually went for Barbie, too, except that one time in the Dream Camper!

The first thing I noticed this day was that there were a lot of large groups walking. Some of them even had matching shirts and neck tags, and buses dropped them off and picked them up along the way. There were also large groups of Spanish students and cyclists whizzing past.

It was time to adjust and accept things. Who cared if there were so many people walking now? Who cared if they were just walking from Sarria? I had been just as excited and fresh as them when I left St Jean. So I decided to focus on the positive; how cool was it that my sister and I were walking on the Camino together?

Had the meaning of the Christian pilgrimage been lost on many of us who did the long Camino Frances from St Jean I wondered? Most of us just loved nature and wanted to hike through a well-maintained hiking area and visit the beautiful Spanish medieval cities. We might peek our heads in a church once in a while to make sure we got a bit of religion on the way, but that wasn't why many people walked. Mostly, I think we liked the social aspect of the Camino. The newness and excitement of every day was addicting.

While pondering my 'deep' thoughts, a Galician bag-piper, clad in traditional clothing, appeared out of nowhere, busking happily in the middle of a pasture. (Where else did you get an opportunity to experience this!) He seemed to be collecting a decent amount of money, as everyone wanted their picture taken with him. It put a nice Celtic swirl on that part of the day. Would a real pilgrim be grateful or mortified by the sight?

Soon after, we made it to the 100 km left to go to Santiago marker. I could not believe that was all there was left now.

The terrain was uphill for about 3 hours and then a gradual descent for 2-1/2 hours. Welcome to the Camino, Sharlene! It amazed me that we walked right through some farms, sometimes in between the house and the barn, dodging cow poop along the way today. I would get sick of people walking past my house all day long.

Somewhere we stopped at a roadside souvenir shop that

had colorfully painted scallop shells lining a wall. We decided not on a shell but on some ice cream instead—a bold choice.

We made a few more pit stops for drinks and snacks but mostly meandered through the rolling hills, flowering bushes, and farmyards that we passed by. It was a beautiful walk, mainly on a natural path through oak and pine forests.

The lingering memory of the day will be the fresh manure —that sweet smell of cow paddies hanging in the air that lasted all day long. And, I had only just washed all my clothes! Aw, the sweet perfume of the countryside.

Getting near to Portomarin, we were faced with a sign that notified us of some different routes. We decided to follow some other people, and it turned out we had taken the more difficult historical shortcut into Portomarin. It was a harrowing, nearly vertical descent down a narrow and rocky path. That scary scramble went down over rocks of irregular shapes and sizes. It was so steep at some points we were sitting down and sliding on our butts for some of it. It would have been dangerous if the rocks had been wet. But we made it!

"So, I joked, "That was an easy bit. Have you been doing a lot of training?"

"Haha, very funny. I didn't exactly see you leaping from rock to rock either. Yes, I've been walking a lot, but my feet are aching!"

"Don't worry; they'll get better. Tylenol and wine help!"

Once we got to Portomarin- and crossed the narrow, slightly scary river bridge over the River Mio, the air seemed to clear, and we could breathe deeply again! However, there was one last test. A final obstacle of a stairway to heaven into town. 52 final steps. We took a few deep breaths and powered up. What a good cardio workout this day had been.

It was a nice view from the top, looking down at the river and reservoir below. Much of town had been dismantled in the 60s brick by brick and relocated up on the hill. If the river was low, you could still see some roofs of the old buildings.

The church bricks in the square had been numbered, so it was easy to put it back together after it had been moved.

As luck would have it, we were staying at Casona Da Ponte just at the top of the steps. It was a newish hotel with dorms and rooms. I kept thinking I was in Greece with all the white-washed buildings here. There was definitely the feeling of being a tourist on vacation here.

After soaking our aching feet for a bit, we found some outdoor cafes and a small town square with pilgrims sitting around. No doubt they had already viewed the church. That would explain the proliferation of gin and tonics on the tables.

We ordered off the pilgrim's meal and had pork chops, and salmon and Raymond joined us for part of the dinner.

"So, how was the first day of the Sister Act? Lots of singing? Were the hills alive?" he joked.

"No singing, but lots of rest stops. We both have sore feet."

"How are your feet doing, Raymond?" I asked him. I knew he had been taping them up every day since back in Belorado.

"They'll get me there." Raymond had a huge backpack, and I don't think he had lightened it much along the way. He carried many art supplies to paint cats and a few of the people of the Camino.

One afternoon, in some town after Logrono, I had been resting on a bench with Lina and Maeve, and he had asked if he could sketch us. We had agreed but didn't know we would be there for over an hour. So we waited (a little impatiently) while he drew us, our poles lying beside us, packs on the ground, and our minds on where we still had to walk to.

Later, he showed us the sketch. He had drawn us each with a tired expression, looking in different directions. It was our eyes that stood out, however. He had made them much larger than they were, so it seemed as if we had a feeling of exceptional excitement and wonder about the day. And I suppose we were still very eager to see what the day had to offer, despite our tiredness. Each day on the Camino was so different. I took a photo of the 'big-eyed' sketch. It's another unique gift of the Camino.

"I'll see you both tomorrow," Raymond said as he walked off after dinner. "Make sure Shannon lets you stop once in a while!"

"I will!"

"Let's just have a little more wine," I suggested.

"I won't say no. It's good for my feet," she giggled.

We enjoyed sitting there for quite a while in that little square as the light faded, gazing up at the church that had been moved brick by brick and looking over at the many pilgrims who had walked there, step by step.

30

THE YELLOW BRICK ROAD

DAY 30- PORTOMARIN TO PALAS DE REI- 25KM

"There was nowhere to go but everywhere." - *Jack Kerouac*

Well, today was a day spent following the long and winding yellow brick road a little closer to the Oz-like Santiago. A light mist hung in the air as we passed through forests of pine and eucalyptus and fields, and then things cleared as we went up and up and up for over an hour. Sharlene was doing better than me with my sore foot. I called myself Thumper - as I slammed my left foot down hard. People could hear me coming. It seemed like it was some sort of arch problem, but I was pretty sure that I could make it to Santiago. I'd crawl if I had to.

We began to notice these fascinating long box-like containers that rested on pillars this day. Some were made of stone, some of wood, and some had little doors built into them. There were often designs on them, and many had little tiled roofs. Some were even decorated with crosses and looked like miniature churches. They seemed to be everywhere, in towns, in fields or even on the side of a winding road. What were they?

Our guidebook, once again had the answer to the mystery of what's in the box? They were called *"horreas,"* and were unique Galician storage containers for grain or other food that needed storage. The fact that they were off the ground kept many rodents away. It was comforting to know the John Brierley always had the answers.

After Mr. Brierley, my person-of-the day would have to be Tim from Berlin, a burnt-out German social worker who was easing down the road after doing a couple of other Caminos. He had started in Grenada and planned to go do the Camino Portuguese after a few days in Santiago.

We stopped for lunch with him and Raymond and a few other people that had been drawn to him. The cheese sandwiches and cervezas with Tim the Camino King were a highlight of this day. He had walked such a great distance and was still going further. He was very inspirational and had sensational tunes!

He was tall with a Jesus beard, wore a hipster fedora, and spoke elegant English with a German tinge. On his back he carried a framed pack with a large sleeping bag and ground roll, and 2 speakers dangled from the bottom. (He seemed to have a preference for The Specials and The Kinks) He blasted music and you heard him coming long before you saw him.

"I want to do this the rest of my life," he told us between bites of a bocadilla and sips of a beer. "I've been walking for a few months now, and I do not want to stop."

"It must be expensive, though?"

"I camp a lot and stay in donativos and the cheapest places I can find. And, I think I will volunteer somewhere."

Tim was a happy German guy, the complete opposite of the unhappy Dutch hippy I initially met. The difference was that Tim was a very social, very friendly guy who attracted people to him. He had an unmistakeable, "joie de vivre." that was contagious. We walked in a large group for quite a while listening to Tim's upbeat music and coasting along on his positive vibes.

I asked for his photo before we separated, and my iPhoto live recorded his words.

"One picture with the King of the Camino," he said.

"It's an honour," I'd replied laughing.

We never saw him again, but I like to think that he is still walking the Camino too, with his tunes, his smile, and his positivity.

It was a beautiful walk this day through colored trees and gorgeous green vistas. Sharlene and I planned to stop in Ventas de Narón, at a former hospital of the Knights Templar. I had read that a blind priest had a cool Knights Templar sello (stamp), and I wanted to get one for my credential. However, I completely forgot about it.

The route also went through so many picture-perfect towns. Somewhere, I believe it was just after crossing the Rio Pambre we had a coffee and a toilet break at the Albergue Santa Domingo. There is a huge scallop shell outside of the building, which was a good draw for many people to stop here.

We ordered some Santiago cake for the first time here. This almond flavored cake was dusted with powdered sugar around the outline of the cross of St. James. The recipe dated back to the Middle Ages and tasted delicious with our cafe con leche.

We got into Palas de Rei about four and spent some time at the square by Buen Camino albergue. The sangria was so delicious here, and many pilgrims were sitting in the sun, happy to have arrived. We were too!

Dinner was at the highly-rated Pulperia a Nosa Terra. Here, we had a couple of good salads, the famous octopus, a fabulous cheese platter, and delicious Padrón peppers. Eating these peppers was a fun experience, as we didn't know which of them might be super hot until we bite into one of them. That's why they were sometimes referred to as the Russian roulette peppers. We survived, as we had quite a lot of Sangria on hand to put out the fire in our mouths if need be.

"Do you remember that guy we saw walking barefoot today," Sharlene said at dinner. "Do you think he trained for that before he came here?"

"Ha, I doubt it. Why? Are you planning to go barefoot tomorrow?"

"No chance, I'd be worried about stepping in all that manure in the towns we walked through today."

"It would feel nice squishing between your toes, though," I suggested with a smirk.

"Maybe, but I'm not doing it! My shoes are nice and comfortable."

"Mine aren't comfortable, and I'm still not doing it," I said. "A lot of people do it for a close connection the road, and to the past, but I think you have to be very committed and tough. I couldn't do it."

We walked back uphill to our hotel a little later, looking at pieces of glass and garbage on the ground with new eyes, imagining what it would be like for a barefoot walker to make those connections to the earth.

31

SOMETIMES WALLS ARE NOT ENOUGH

DAY 31- PALAS DE REI TO RIBADISO-27 KM

"Go as far as you can see; when you get there you'll be able to see farther"-Thomas Carlyle

. . .

The day's walk started in fields of wild mint and forests of eucalyptus. Cuckoos, cats, and cows sang to the sun, and we felt more lively than the day before.

Today we had a hotel reserved in Ribadiso, which was a pretty small place. It looked like there were two hotels, one restaurant, and no shop. However, we were surrounded by cow pastures and lovely black and white cows strolling around power-munching on some grass and that sweet cow aroma once again.

Our walking clothes were washed out and hanging on the line for the next day. We were pretty exhausted after the walking game of uphill then downhill and didn't get in till almost 5. We were so glad we hadn't reserved in Arzua, which though it was a bigger place, would have been another 5 km. Ribadiso was far enough.

The previous night had not been great. The walls at the hotel had been paper-thin. A French guy, in the room next door, was talking loudly on his cell phone till after midnight. What an inconsiderate jerk! He spoke too fast, and I couldn't even eavesdrop on his conversation. I could tell that he was not happy though, because he was shouting at the person on the other end.

Thinking good Camino thoughts, I'd pounded loudly on the wall several times.

"Please, be quiet! It's after midnight."

"Enough!" he'd yelled back at me.

"Shut up," I tried again.

"Enough!" he yelled again. What did that even mean?

I decided I had better not pursue it. I didn't want him pounding on our door.

So then I angrily and accidentally threw the remote on the tile floor a few times. That made quite a satisfying sound.

Then I'd turned on the TV at full volume and slammed some more things around. It made me feel better, but it was useless. He just talked louder.

At 1 am, he got guests. Things got even louder. Somehow we drifted off to sleep in the middle of the night.

In the morning, we were exhausted. I got some degree of satisfaction, slamming our door shut as we went downstairs for breakfast. I also stomped loudly on the marble floor in front of his room—there was an excellent echo. I know I should have gone full Camino and turned the other cheek—but I was a bit grumpy from the lack of much sleep.

We ran down to the breakfast room before he opened the door. There were a few other people already sitting at tables, sipping on coffee and eating toast.

A noisy bunch of guys came downstairs in their tight tiny Spandex bike shorts and sports shirts. I was pretty sure I knew what room they were staying in.

"Don't look at them," Sharlene whispered.

"They don't know what we look like."

"I know, but we are the only women here. They might figure it out!"

We ate breakfast in exhausted silence. I glared at them on the way out. They glared back, the shiny Spandex highlighting their tired red eyes. At least they hadn't gotten much sleep either.

If only I could have spilled some coffee near them, I would have felt even better.

So, with some blurry vision, we trudged upward into a lovely forest area to do some therapeutic tree-bathing. I'd read that walking in forests (fully clothed, of course) is excellent for your health; trees release some relaxing substances that make you feel better. It took a while (like all morning), but I eventually forgot about that hotel room neighbour.

It was a day of trees today. I think we saw oak, poplar, pine trees, and eucalyptus, among others whose names I don't know. The up and downhill among the different trees continued all day. Sometimes it seemed like we were walking through enchanted forests with thick, mossy branches hanging heavily above us. They gave a real Alice in Wonderland feel to the day!

"In a forest of a hundred thousand trees, no two leaves are alike. And no two journeys along the same path are alike". (Paulo Coelho).

I was thinking about this as we walked the different forests today. Everyone is here for a different reason, but we are all walking the same, Camino.

So, after the soothing tree bathing, chatting with people on group tours, and other solo walkers, many of us stopped for the day in Ribadiso and are saving the uphill for the morning.

We ordered the ever-present versatile chicken off the pilgrim's menu and watched (and listened to!) a sturdy young man drive his tractor up and down the one main street repeatedly. I think he was hauling water but may have been trying to attract attention. Date night in Ribadiso, perhaps? But, unfortunately, it seemed like this was the only action in town!

The albergue here was in a renovated 15th century Pilgrim's hospital. After a long day of walking, it looked like a good place to dangle your feet in the river, as pilgrims did so many years ago. It seemed too cold for us!

32

OUT OF THE SHADOWS

DAY 32- RIBADISO-O PEDROUZO-24 KM

"The woods are lovely, dark and deep. But I have promises to keep, and miles to go before I sleep." – Robert Frost

. . .

Yes, it had been a much quieter night! We set off refreshed at 7:30 and got to O Pedrouzo by 3 pm.

All day long, there had been inspirational signposts. "You're nearly there!" and "Your destiny is waiting for you."

We began to see the lines of John Lennon's song "Imagine" written on walls, signs and garbage cans by the side of the trail. We found ourselves anticipating the next lines, and we even started singing the chorus long before we could see the writing. Good thing there was no one around! Yes, sometimes it is the simple things that make those special memories.

In one quiet little town, we came upon a wonderful word collection called "The Wall of Wisdom." It was simply a bunch of random ideas that someone had printed on construction paper, laminated, and lined up on display on an old wall for pilgrims to read and contemplate during their walk past. My favorite was, "Has religion had a positive or negative impact on our society?"

Soon after, we found a neat stop at A Calle, where we stopped to take pictures at the Casa Tia Dolores. We drank a few bottles of Peregrina (Pilgrim) Beer, then wrote our names, hometown, and a wish on the bottle. Older bottles were displayed on tree branches, doors, and tables. I hope ours made it to a well-positioned tree branch. The fun never stopped on the Camino! There were masses of bottles and a very happy group of Spaniards leading some community singing. Where had they been when we needed help with the chorus from "Imagine."

It was a day of inspiration, reflection, and, yes, perspiration too. The many rest stops made it an easy day, though.

The last part of the day was in a lovely forested area that seemed to go on and on. It felt like we should have arrived, and then we noticed it sure was taking a long time to go the last 5 km. We were following a couple of other people and watched, horrified, as they turned around. Uh Oh! Yes, we had all missed an arrow, missed the town, and walked a lot of extra kilometers. At least now I could say that I did get lost on the Camino at least once!

O Pedrouzo was a weird little place. There was just a short main street with all the cafes and albergues located here. We arrived at the albergue with sore feet but also had some fluffy towels and a hairdryer available for use at the reception.

A cheap dollar store near our hotel was doing a humming business selling cheap Camino souvenirs to pilgrims. It really seemed like we were getting close to the end.

Dinner was pizza and sangria at a small table on the street, and that seemed like the choice for most people. A tired old man, wearing faded, ripped clothes, approached us with a newspaper clipping about himself that had been written many years ago. He spoke Spanish, and the clipping was in Spanish also, but I could guess at its contents. He had walked the Camino many times and had become a little famous from it. But, now, sadly, he went from table to table showing his clipping and collecting a little money here and there.

We gave him a bit of money and watched as other people did too. Of course, he reminded me of Angelina and Tomasso.

And so, dinner had been eaten; sangria had been drunk, bags had been packed for the morning sprint into Santiago. It was about 20 km and would take 4-5 hours depending upon how many times we stopped. I wanted to make it by 12:30, as Lina had texted me that she would be catching a bus to the airport about then) I hoped that we could get there in time for me to say goodbye.

I knew that arriving in Santiago would seem surreal. The cathedral area would be full of pilgrims arriving and taking photos. There would be a feeling of relief that we all had made it- and sadness that it was all over. It would be quite the morning! The guidebook said, "Prepare for large crowds and create an air of compassionate detachment." "Be patient and prepare for a long slog up to Mount Gozo."

All that remained was the end. What would it be like?

33

SOUL SEARCHING IN SANTIAGO
DAY 33-O PEDROUZO TO SANTIAGO-20KM

"Don't cry because it's over, smile because it happened."— *Dr. Seuss*

I hardly know how to start about today. How do you tell a story about the end?

Sometimes I never thought that it would end. Sometimes I wanted it to, and sometimes I did not. What was left to remember; the pain, the laughter, and the tears? Should I burn my boots? Stick someone with my poles? Empty the contents of my bag in front of the cathedral?

I remember the words of *The Weight,* from the group The Band, were ringing in my head when Sharlene and I pulled into Santiago at about half-past 12. We were feeling about half-past dead for sure. But, we had arrived—and yes, we had a bed!

My sister was a little Energizer bunny. She took a 'licking and kept on ticking!' From Sarria, she had just jumped into this journey with me and scoffed at the blisters, sore feet, and yes, even no hair-dryers. It was not an easy walk from Sarria, and we had finished it off together!

We'd left about 7 am and walked at a pretty good clip; I believe flames may have been shooting out our heels as well as our butts! A lot of the day was in and out of industrial zones and past the occasional farmhouse. Unlike the day before, there weren't a lot of coffee stops. What few that were open were filled with exhausted pilgrims and people desperate for those last stamps.

We got down the hill and onto the highway where the famed "Santiago" sign was. We dodged some cars and many lanes of traffic to get our photos taken in front of the sign. It had to be done.

Somewhat miraculously, we made it into Santiago before noon. As we walked down the ancient archway into the plaza, bagpipes played, and then we walked around a bit more. Where was the plaza? I texted the ladies, and it appeared we were at the wrong plaza. They were waiting at the main plaza. Who gets lost coming into Santiago?

We walked around, past groups of school children and tour groups, and then finally, there it was the holy cathedral of Santiago- in all its scaffolded glory.

There were people everywhere, hugging, crying, and simply sitting. And then I spotted my two ladies; we couldn't miss them. We had all been wearing the same clothes for the past month. There was Maeve's blue shirt and Lina's brown jacket!

It was fantastic that Lina and Maeve met us at the Cathedral, and I felt a great sense of closure. I began the walk with these ladies and was able to see them at the conclusion also. It just seemed right!!

I introduced my sister to them, and it almost seemed like the four of us had walked the whole way together. We were all so happy to be in Santiago. My sister and Maeve talked a bit, and Lina called me over.

"We got bedbugs in Astorga," she whispered.

"What! Where did you stay?"

"One of those municipal albergues. I think the blankets had the bedbugs. We both had so many itchy red bites in the morning.

"How did you get rid of them?"

"We got a hotel room, and then we went to a laundromat and washed everything even the backpacks, and just wore shorts and t-shirt in the room till things were dry.

"Did it work?"

"Yes, we didn't have any more trouble. But, Maeve was angry at the albergue."

"Did you go back and tell them?"

"Yes, but they didn't believe us."

"That's terrible. I'm so sorry to hear that, but I'm glad you got rid of the bugs."

"Maeve doesn't want anyone to know, so please keep it a secret."

"OK, but I think it's not so bad. A lot of people get bedbugs."

"I know, but Maeve didn't want to. I think it ruined the last few weeks for her. She was always worried about getting them again."

"That really sucks, but I guess you had the full Camino experience, even if you didn't want it ."

We rejoined Sharlene and Maeve, took a few photos, and reminisced a bit about our first night all together in Zubiri. The two German girls, Laura and Anna, had been following my blog and had let me know they had arrived in Santiago a few days before. I was glad to know that they had made it also.

Lina, Maeve, and I remembered it all. Some great meals, wonderful scenery, creaky bunk beds, and outstanding people we had met. Sometimes we had got on each other's nerves, but don't all 'families' have this problem? Nobody brought up Angelina's name.

Finally, we all walked Lina to the bus to the airport and waved her bus off. I shed a few tears as she waved from inside the bus. We were a long way from Gite Makila now. Those red curtains had been open for a long time.

My sister and I had a reservation at the Parador, and there would be time for a long hot bath and some big goopy swirls of conditioner for the hair. And fluffy towels. Lots of fluffy towels.

What a place! It was supposedly the oldest hotel in the world and was conveniently located right across from the Cathedral. Once, it had been a pilgrims' hospital and was now it was a luxurious hotel.

By royal charter, this Parador had to continue offering hospitality to pilgrims and provide food to 10 pilgrims every breakfast, lunch, and dinnertime. Of course, they had to line up at a special entrance and not eat in the main dining room, but still, this was a good motivation for some pilgrims to get up early in Santiago.

Suddenly in the square near the Parador, I saw two more familiar heads. Christina and Ingrid were here too! They were crying, hugging and taking photos.

And, then another familiar face-Raymond!

"We made it!" we all cried together and took many, many photos.

I was so happy to run into everyone. We all decided to have a farewell dinner together. There was a lot of laughter and the sharing of good memories. Christina gifted me with a special Leipzig flag which was close to her heart. She and I had a great Camino connection, and I expect to see her on another Camino one day!

It was a fantastic feeling to have completed this walk. I had started the journey alone, but I had finished with friends. Finally, I had found the community I had been looking for on the Camino.

I knew some people felt grief and sadness and great joy at the conclusion in Santiago. But I just felt happy, really, really happy. I didn't feel sad at all. It was lovely to have this celebration of reaching our destination to share with my Camino family and a part of my real family, my sister. There was nothing that any of us could put into words there, yet, we all felt it. It was that feeling of completion of being able to share this magical moment.

I came on this journey to find out if I was still strong enough to be alone and depend on myself. I'd had 35 days to contemplate life, and you know what I figured out? I was happy in my skin, on my own feet, blisters and warts and all.

34

TO THE FIELD OF STARS

DAY 34-SANTIAGO TO FINISTERRE

"Not just beautiful, though — the stars are like the trees in the forest, alive and breathing. And they're watching me."- Haruki Murakami

There was one more place to visit, but we didn't have time to walk. So we took the bus tour to Finisterre and Muxia and thought that it was fabulous. It made plenty of stops, and we had the luxury of time this day trip. We ducked down every time we saw pilgrims walking along the road, though.

The drive went along the Coast of Death; called so because of the many shipwrecks over the years. You could see why because it was very rocky!!

At Finisterre (From the Latin "Finis Terrae"- Land's End), we had reached the natural end of the world. There was no place left to walk from here. The pilgrims of long ago would reach this point and symbolically burn possessions they no longer wanted. We saw some evidence of a few modern-day fires among the rocks too. But it was just a place to stand by the sea and realize there was no place left to walk.

We had a nice lunch at an open-air seafood restaurant and felt like we were no longer pilgrims. Instead, we were tourists for the day.

The walk to Finisterre is 3-4 days from Santiago, should you choose to follow the last stars of the Milky Way to the 'end of the world.'

Many pilgrims were faced with the prospect of turning around and walking home from here long ago. Some took a Galician scallop shell from the beach as evidence of their walk. If this is true, that over a million pilgrims walked the Camino in the Middle Ages, that is a heck of a lot of missing shells from the beaches!

The scallop shell, if examined closely, also has a special meaning, according to many people. All the grooves on the shell come together at an endpoint on the shell, and many people believe this is a metaphor for the different routes on the Camino. Nine routes meet in Santiago, each line represented on the shell.

We got back to town at 6 pm and then raced over to the pilgrim office to get our Compostelas and distance certificates. The stamps in my Pilgrim credential were examined to prove that I had come all the way from St Jean. I loved to look at all those stamps of places like Pamplona, Foncebadon, O Cebreiro, Leon, and so many others, and remember those days.

A volunteer then carefully wrote my name on a special piece of paper. It was my Compostela; written in a beautiful colourful Latin script. It was so gratifying to receive this certificate. I bought a red tube to store it in at the small shop, and it felt like I was carrying a sword in my hand.

I knew that many people framed their credentials and Compostelas once they got home, and perhaps I would too.

Later, standing out in the square surrounded by many new pilgrims still arriving, I said goodbye to Maeve. It is her that I shall remember the most from these days on the Camino. I never really cracked her shell, and I suppose that she never really cracked mine either.

"Well, we made it," she said.

"Yes, we did. It was a little tougher than I thought it would be. It was so lovely to walk so far with you, Maeve."

"I enjoyed every day Shannon. Come visit me in Ireland if you're ever there!" And then she was off too. She was headed by bus for a few days to relax in Porto.

She saw the world in black and white, and I was looking for the color, I think. She quietly encouraged me and challenged me along the way. She was an exceptional person, and we still keep in touch. I hope we always will.

35

THE END OF THE ROAD

DAY 35-SANTIAGO

"The miracle is not to walk on water. The miracle is to walk on the green earth, dwelling deeply in the present moment and feeling truly alive"-Thích Nhất Hạnh

. . .

This was our final day in Spain; it was hard to believe! Everyone we knew had moved on, and Sharlene and I had the day to explore. The square in front of the Cathedral was enormous; there were no bars and no shops here. It was just a vast empty space that filled up with full of people completing their journey, looking up in awe at the Cathedral and surrounding buildings. Some people sat down and cried, some ran to hug newly arrived friends, some threw their bags in the air, and some simply stood and quietly watched the moments of pure joy and even disbelief on display everywhere beside the Cathedral.

Because of its history as a destination for pilgrims since medieval times, the old city is full of ancient monasteries, convents, and hospitals. Many are now converted to hotels, university buildings, schools, restaurants, and museums. The whole of one side of the cathedral square is taken up by our ✓ Parador, which we loved staying at. Further away are winding mazes of narrow streets, cute restaurants and plenty of souvenir shops for those wishing a final silver scallop shell, an "I Walked the Camino" t-shirt, or some boxed Santiago cake to take home.

We finally visited the jewel of Santiago—the Cathedral this day. The most famous building in Santiago towered above us, its facade draped in netting and scaffolds. Even though the Cathedral was closed for repairs, parts of it were open during the restoration work. But, oh my gosh, there were just hordes of tour groups there this morning. There was nothing we could do but join the line.

Inside was a collection of gold plated sculptures, intricate woodwork and beautiful stained glass, like many of the churches on the Camino. This one seemed infinitely more crowded, more ornate, and much, much important. An all-knowing and watchful eye looked down from the center of the ceiling. And behind the altar was a statue of St James himself, made of gold and emblazoned with jewels; eye-catching and unforgettable.

We followed the hundreds of people and shuffled around looking at the altar, the burning candles, and feeling humbled. I could see how utterly fantastic it would have been to attend a service there. Over a thousand pilgrims attended when it was open, and a "Botafumeiro" swung over the congregation dispersing smoky air and blessing those assembled. But, today, with the scaffolding covering many of the ornate gold carvings, and no scheduled services for quite some time, it just wasn't the same.

We joined a long queue to hug the statue of St James and then stepped into the crypt where his martyred remains are supposed to lie. For thousands of pilgrims, reaching this hallowed ground is the entire reason for walking the Camino.

We saw the tomb of St. James in all its Catholic glory. It was down several steps to a tiny room, and many people stood in a queue, gazing at the shiny silver box that was not much bigger than a child's coffin. Hanging above it was a nice shiny, silver star and in front were perfect red roses. A spotlight shone on the box, which gave it a sense of celebrity and even more importance. I stood there looking at the box and thinking about how I wasn't feeling anything. Nothing at all.

This was because I didn't actually believe that St. James was in the box. And even if somehow he was, being physically close to body parts does nothing for me. Zilch. Relics were not the reason I'd come to Santiago.

I think the experience of the spiritual portion of the Camino is in watching the fields awaken in the breeze, listening to leaves rustling in the eucalyptus, smelling the earthy air, looking at the lush green of the hills and the blood-red of the poppies, and so much more, with big wondering eyes, just as Raymond had sketched us one day.

Finally, this day, we moved onto the Spanish Pilgrim Mass, which was temporarily being celebrated at the San Francisco church just down the street from the Cathedral. There were at least 500 people from all over the world there for the 12:00 mass. If you have done the Camino, it is worthwhile attending. Full communion is offered if you are Catholic, or you can simply receive a blessing. A small portion was in English, wishing all pilgrims a safe journey back to our countries and to continue to keep Christ in our hearts wherever we go.

It was special and meaningful, and I felt like this journey was complete after the Mass today.

Like all of us who had reached Santiago knew, there is no way to explain this experience to people at home.

AFTERWORD

Every time I look at the palm of my hand, I remember my Camino. The deeply grooved lines are still there, moving from east to west.

All of us who walk the Camino year after year constantly change it. We have new experiences which become whispers and then new stories themselves. The Camino is the story of tens of thousands of people who walk alone and in small groups, suffering through the pains and experiencing joy and a sense of community. This was what the Camino meant to me.

I stopped at all the well-known albergues and followed most of the suggested stages of walking.However, there are thousands of other places to stay and special places that I hope to find next time. Perhaps they are not as well known, but they are just as magical, unique, and a part of the Camino.

My Camino journey was not quite done. I met Maeve in Dublin a few months later. I was in the country with my family and arranged a meeting at Bewley's, a famous cafe on Grafton Street. It was odd to see each other outside of Spain, and I was a little worried that we would have nothing to say to each other. But, the words flowed, and though we had many differences, we could just pick up where we left off.

She had wanted to show me the National Museum of Ireland, and we went there together after our coffee. The extensive collection included beautiful jewelry, art, weapons, and everyday items of the Celts. The gold collection was stunning, and it made me wonder what might be lying underneath the cobblestones up in O Cebreiro. I was so happy that we were able to share one more experience together. And, so I said goodbye to Maeve, my Celtic connector, one more time. I hope it was not the last.

I had a letter once from Angelina. She is still on the Camino, somewhere walking west, volunteering where she can. I think it is the only place that truly feels like home for her.

She doesn't need more than she has. Her load is light, and the Way is easy for her.

I still have my copy of *On The Road*, which traveled back from Spain with me. It sits on the shelf with many Camino books.

I try to walk every day to keep the feel of the Camino in me and keep the lessons of the road alive. The road I followed has already faded; the feet of a few hundred thousand pilgrims made sure of that. The places on the Camino are just memories now, and there is nothing wrong with that.

Remembering it all, I can feel the whispering traces of another time, of more determined pilgrims who walked hundreds of miles to the 'end of the earth' to know what it was to struggle and overcome in the company of strangers.

There are so many reminders of the Camino scratched in my heart — memories, friendships, and an inspired approach to life. I have tried to maintain the spirit and simplicity of the Camino. But, it's hard when surrounded by so many distractions and consumerism, and yes, Netflix. I can see why people keep coming back to the Camino, again and again, and again!

I, too, have succumbed to the Santiago syndrome of thinking and dreaming of the Camino all the time. It is a simpler life, in a kinder and gentler place, that brings out the best in all of us.

I believe that the Camino still allows pilgrims to find the magic in the mundane. It is the small moments on this 'wanderful' walk that take you by surprise. The Camino is all about tasting colors and touching sounds; trying things differently. If we can live our lives in colour we can truly become Camino chameleons! Buen Camino!!

.

RECIPES FROM THE ROAD

Santiago Cake

Nobody knows where the first recipes for Santiago cake came from, but perhaps the cake was brought to Galicia by a pilgrim and heartily (and happily!) consumed by those making the journey to the cathedral.

An outline of the cross of St. James on the top, is what makes this cake special. But, you could literally put anything you wanted on the top even a maple leaf!

It is a simple and delicious cake to prepare and will keep your memories of the Camino alive!

Ingredients
- 4 eggs
- 1 cup sugar
- 2 cups almond flour
- 1 lemon zest
- ½ tsp cinnamon
- icing sugar (approx) to dust on top of cake
. 3-4 drops almond extract

Instructions
- Preheat your oven to 350F. Line an 8 inch cake tin with parchment paper. Grease the sides with a little butter.
- Crack the eggs into a bowl and add in the sugar. Whisk the two together.
- Add the almond flour, lemon zest and cinnamon. Mix well.
- Pour the mixture into the cake tin and put in the preheated oven. Bake for approximately 30 minutes. See if its is done by inserting a skewer in the middle until it comes out clean.

Prepare the cross stencil, which can be found on internet.
- Remove the cake from the oven and allow to cool about 10-15 minutes on a cooling rack before removing from the tin. Allow it to cool completely before placing the stencil on top and then dusting some icing sugar over the top. Slice and enjoy!

Natillas
Ingredients
- 2 cups milk
- 1/2 cup sugar (or substitute like monk fruit sweetener)
- 1 tablespoon cornstarch dissolved in water
- 1 teaspoon vanilla extract
- 2 egg yolks slightly beaten
- pinch of salt
- cinnamon
- 4 Sweet Marie cookies (or more if desired!)

Instructions
- Combine everything in a large saucepan and cook over medium heat .
- Stir constantly until it comes to a boil.
- Pour the custard through a strainer into dessert cups.
- Sprinkle the top with cinnamon and place 2 Sweet Marie cookies in the custard.

Caldo Gallego
Ingredients:
1/2 pound of chopped bacon
2 large potatoes cut into 1 inch cubes
2 cloves of garlic chopped
1 bay leaf
2 large cans of kidney beans
8 cups of water or chicken broth
1 large onion diced
1 large sliced sausage
1 lb chopped kale
2 tbsp olive oil

Instructions:
Saute the bacon and sausage in the olive oil until a little crispy. Add the onions, garlic and bay leaf. Cook the onions for a few minutes.

Remove the sausage to add later. Add the water or broth, potatoes, and the kale .

Let the soup cook on low for about 1 hour. Add the beans and the sausage. Stir and cook for another 30 minutes on low heat.

Remove the bay leaf and add more olive oil as a garnish before serving.

Padron Peppers

These small peppers are definitely becoming more accessible in the USA. Peppers from Padrón, come in a small package and some are very hot and some are not. These small green peppers, make an exciting, unpredictable dining experience. Think Russian roulette, but with spicy peppers! What could be more fun!

Ingredients

Bag of Padron Peppers

Instructions

1 Heat a bit of olive oil in a large skillet over high heat.

2 Add the peppers and let them cook about 5 minutes per side, until the skin starts to blister up.

3 When they're done and the skins are blistered, toss them with a bit of sea salt and freshly squeezed lime juice.

4. Choose carefully. Do you like hot or not?

Mixed Tuna Salad
Ingredients
2 large eggs (boiled)
1 head romaine or iceberg lettuce
2 medium tomatoes
1 medium cucumber
1 medium red or yellow bell pepper
1/4 red onion
1 medium carrot
1 (6-ounce) can tuna
1 (15-ounce) can white asparagus (hard to find!)
1/2 cup olives (pitted black olives work best)
1 (15-ounce) can baby corn, drained

3 tablespoons extra-virgin olive oil
1 tablespoon red wine (or balsamic vinegar)

Cut, and mix as you like. A great filling salad!

Galician Sangria
Ingredients
1 750 Bottle of Red Spanish Wine (or any red!)
1 Lemon
1 Orange
1 Peach
1 Apple
1/4 cup Spanish Brandy (yes, or any Brandy!)
1 cup Orange Juice
1/3 Cup White Sugar (or monk fruit sweetener)
1 Cinnamon Stick

Instructions
1 Thinly slice 1 orange and 1 lemon, add half of the

orange slices and half of the lemon slices into a pitcher and save the other slices. Cut 1 peach and 1 apple into small pieces and add all the peaches and half the apples to the pitcher.

2 Next add a 1/4 cup of a brandy into the pitcher, 1 cup of orange juice (freshly squeezed is best!) and 1/3 cup of white sugar (or sweetener).

3 Using a large wooden spoon, crunch down on the fruit to release all the juices and then mix everything together.

4 Now add one 750 ml bottle of red wine into the pitcher, (Rioja wine is a popular choice!) then add 1 cinnamon stick, mix everything together and add the pitcher to the fridge for a few hours (if you can wait!)

5 When ready to serve, stir the sangria around in the pitcher, then add some ice cubes. Garnish with more fresh fruit!

6. Grab another bottle of wine and try again!

THE THINGS I CARRIED

- Small back-pack
    - down-filled jacket
    - hiking shoes
    - light-weight sleeping bag
    - 2 pair wool socks
    - 3 pair underwear
    - 3 light-weight shirts (one long-sleeved, two short-sleeved)
    - raincoat
    - 2 pair hiking pants
    - 1 pair shorts
    - Teva hiking sandals
    - small micro-towel
    - Eagle-creek compression bags
    - hat/buff/gloves for colder weather
    - earplugs
    - A medkit : anti-inflammatory gel, painkillers, Compeed, small sewing kit, chap-stick, sunscreen
    - Lush soap (for showering and hand-washing)
    - sunglasses
    - Camino guidebook
    - Money belt
    - Ziplock bags
    - Earphones
    - Charger and portable charger for daytime

Note: I did not carry a full-pack each day, as I wore pants, shirt etc. Pack weighed under 10% of my body weight.

ACKNOWLEDGMENTS

How can I begin my acknowledgments without first thanking my Camino family? To all the people I met on the path, thank you for it all!

I would also like to thank all those people who encouraged me to remember my Camino back home. I have struggled to get it written, and thanks to my family for insisting.

To my daughter, who continues to support my crazy new hobby of writing. I am immensely proud to be your mom.

To my husband Peter, who lets me walk down any path, supporting me, and listens to my many Camino stories again and again and again. I hope you can join me on the next one.

Thanks also to the many proofreaders who focused their 'new eyes' after my 'big-eyed' writing was done. A special shout-out to my fabulous Beta-Readers: my mom, Sharlene, Jessica and Shae. Thanks for getting me to the finish line!

ABOUT THE AUTHOR

Shannon O'Gorman grew up in Winnipeg, kicking the snow-drifts in the winter and avoiding the mosquitos in the summer. She took her first solo trip to New Zealand and loved the country and traveling so much she has tried never to stop. She currently lives in California with her husband, Peter, and their daughter Jessica, when university is not in session.

ALSO BY SHANNON O'GORMAN

Some Wanderful Times